How to Use
HTML3

How to Use
HTML3

SCOTT ARPAJIAN

Ziff-Davis Press
Emeryville, California

Development Editor	Kelly Green
Copy Editors	Margo Hill and Nicole Clausing
Technical Reviewer	Wayne Ause
Project Coordinator	Ami Knox
Cover Illustration and Design	Regan Honda
Book Design	Dennis Gallagher/Visual Strategies, San Francisco
Screen Graphics Editor	Pipi Diamond
Word Processing	Howard Blechman
Page Layout	M.D. Barrera
Indexer	Valerie Robbins

Ziff-Davis Press, ZD Press, and the Ziff-Davis Press logo are licensed to Macmillan Computer Publishing USA by Ziff-Davis Publishing Company, New York, New York.

Ziff-Davis Press imprint books are produced on a Macintosh computer system with the following applications: FrameMaker®, Microsoft® Word, QuarkXPress®, Adobe Illustrator®, Adobe Photoshop®, Adobe Streamline™, MacLink®*Plus*, Aldus® FreeHand™, Collage Plus™.

If you have comments or questions or would like to receive a free catalog, call or write:
Macmillan Computer Publishing USA
Ziff-Davis Press Line of Books
5903 Christie Avenue
Emeryville, CA 94608
800-688-0448

ISBN 1-56276-390-3

Manufactured in the United States of America
10 9 8 7 6 5 4 3 2

To my grandfather and hero, Stephen Fay, whose creativity and patience always amazes and inspires me

TABLE OF CONTENTS

ACKNOWLEDGMENTS

It's unfortunate that only one name appears in big bold letters on the cover of this book, because in reality, several people are responsible for making it all happen. I'd like to thank everyone at Ziff-Davis Press who had a hand in putting this book together. It's truly a group effort, and everyone involved deserves some of the credit. In particular, I'd like to thank Suzanne Anthony and Kelly Green, whose expertise, patience, good humor, and encouragement kept me sane and helped bring this book to completion. Acknowledgment and thanks for the LawnBirds concept go to Eric Stone. A huge thank-you also goes to Preston Gralla, who originally got me involved in the project and offered advice and wisdom from the very beginning. Finally, I'd like to deeply thank all of my friends, especially Lisa, for their patience, understanding, and support along the way.

INTRODUCTION

 The World Wide Web is exploding all around us, and it shows no signs of slowing down. Chances are that if you've opened the book to this page, you're already familiar with the Internet in general and the World Wide Web in particular. You've probably already explored what the Web has to offer, and like millions of others, you've become hooked by its limitless information and exciting content. In fact, you've probably even thought about publishing your own home page on the Web.

Surprisingly, publishing on the Web is easy. The backbone of the World Wide Web is the Hypertext Markup Language, often simply referred to as HTML. This is the language that is used to create Web pages, and it is the glue that holds all of the pieces of the Web together. Despite its power and flexibility, HTML is simple to understand and write. HTML is not complicated, and it doesn't require special compilers or tools. In fact, you can write HTML just as I did for this book—using the Windows Notepad.

How to Use HTML3 is an illustrated tutorial that will teach you the fundamentals of HTML. It starts with the basics, and then moves on to the more advanced concepts. Along the way, you'll get the chance to practice your skills in a series of exercises known as Try-Its. By the time you complete this book, you'll be an accomplished HTML author. Even when you finish reading the book, you can continue to use it as a reference and guide as you publish your own documents on the Web.

The Web is an exciting medium, and it levels the playing field for electronic publishing. Anyone can publish on the Web. There are very few obstacles, and no special tools are required. All you need is a working knowledge of HTML, some disk space on a Web server, and a whole lot of ambition. This book will teach you everything you need to know about creating HTML content on the World Wide Web. The rest is up to you.

Scott Arpajian
Boston, Massachusetts
E-mail: scott_arpajian@zd.com

CHAPTER 1

Understanding the World Wide Web

One of the best things about the World Wide Web is that it's just as easy to create Web pages as it is to browse them. The key to publishing on the Web is having a firm understanding of Hypertext Markup Language (HTML). Despite the intimidating name, HTML is extremely simple to learn and use. By the time you finish this book, you'll be well on your way to becoming an HTML wizard.

Before diving head-first into the language of HTML itself, it will help you to understand a little bit about how the World Wide Web works. After all, HTML is designed to guide users through the vast and tangled resources of the Web. As an HTML author, you will need to understand some of the basics behind the architecture of the World Wide Web. Knowing how the Web works, as well as when it doesn't and why, can help you make important decisions about how to construct your own Web pages.

It would be impossible to describe in detail the inner workings of the Web in a single chapter. With that in mind, this chapter provides you with a "refresher course" on the basics. Armed with this basic knowledge, you'll be able to move on to writing your own Web pages in a very short time.

How the World Wide Web Works

The World Wide Web is a vast collection of information that is spread across hundreds of thousands of computers around the world. When you access a document on the Web, there's a lot going on behind the scenes. Here's a very simple and brief description.

1 The World Wide Web is a network of thousands of computers, all of which fall neatly into two categories: *clients* and *servers*. Through the use of special software, they form a kind of network called, not surprisingly, a *client-server network*.

6 Most of the documents on the World Wide Web are written in Hypertext Markup Language (HTML). HTML provides instructions for the client software on how the document should be displayed. HTML also contains information about how to link up to other documents on the Web.

TIP SHEET

▶ **Many people consider the World Wide Web and the Internet to be one and the same. The World Wide Web is only part of the Internet, but it's growing at a faster rate than any other part.**

▶ **You can read about how the Internet works in *How to Use the Internet, Second Edition* from Ziff-Davis Press.**

2 Servers store information and process requests from clients. Then they send the requested information to the clients. This information includes all kinds of data, including images, sounds, and text. Servers also send instructions to the client on how to display all this information. These instructions are sent in the form of Hypertext Markup Language (HTML).

3 Clients make requests for information and then handle the chore of displaying that information to the end user. When you are using a Web browser to navigate the Web, your browsing software is acting as a client.

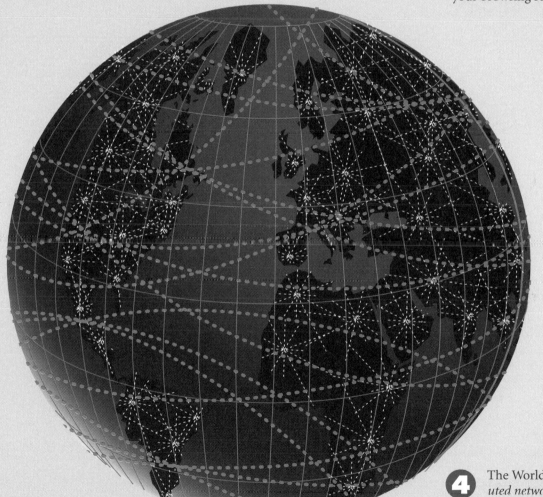

4 The World Wide Web is a *distributed network*. That means there is no central computer for the World Wide Web. Any server on the Web can be accessed directly by any client. If a server on the World Wide Web malfunctions, it doesn't affect the performance of other servers.

5 Users navigate the World Wide Web through the use of hypertext links. When you select or click on a hypertext link, you go to another area on the Internet. Almost all of the documents on the Web are interconnected through the use of hypertext links.

How Do URLs Work?

Almost every item of information on the World Wide Web can be accessed directly. That's because every document, file, and image has a specific address. These addresses are called *Uniform Resource Locators* (URLs). URLs are used by Web browsing software to locate and access information on the World Wide Web. Think of URLs as postal addresses for the Internet.

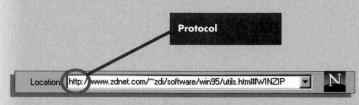

1 The first part of the URL is known as the *protocol*. This is almost always *http://*, which is short for Hypertext Transfer Protocol. Some URLs start with a different protocol, such as *ftp://* or *news://*. If you're accessing a document on your local machine instead of on the Web, the URL will begin with *file://*.

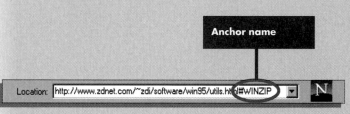

5 Sometimes the URL contains a fifth part, known as the *anchor name*. This is a pointer to a specific part of an HTML document. It's always preceded by the pound sign (#). Anchors are especially useful for large documents.

TIP SHEET

▸ **Be very careful when specifying URLs. The Web is very unforgiving with URLs, and will only accept exact matches. If you receive a "document not found" message when trying to access a page on the Web, make sure the URL is typed in correctly.**

▸ **Most browsers allow you to store your favorite URLs as "bookmarks." Use bookmarks to save yourself the trouble of typing in the full URL each time.**

Domain name

Location: http://www.zdnet.com/~zdi/software/win95/utils.html#WINZIP ▼ N

2 The second part of the URL is known as the *domain name*. If you've used e-mail on the Internet, you're probably already familiar with domains. The domain represents the name of the server that you're connecting to.

Directory path

Location: http://www.zdnet.com/~zdi/software/win95/utils.html#WINZIP ▼ N

3 The third part of the URL is called the *directory path*. This is the specific area on the server where the item resides. Directory paths on Web servers work a lot like they do on your desktop computer. To locate a particular file on a server, you need to indicate its directory path first.

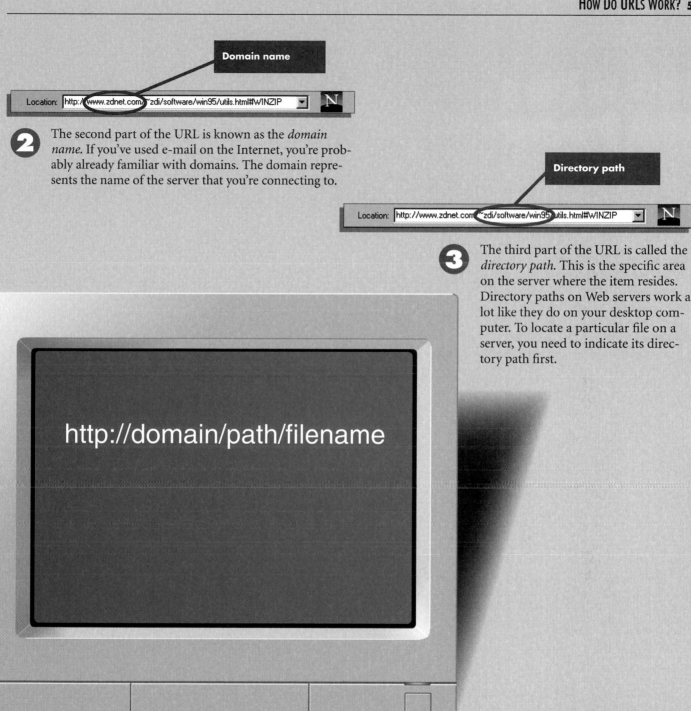

http://domain/path/filename

Document file name

Location: http://www.zdnet.com/~zdi/software/win95/utils.html#WINZIP ▼ N

4 The fourth part of the URL is called the *document file name*. This indicates the specific file being accessed. This is usually an HTML file, but it can also be an image, sound, or another file.

How to Use a Web Browser

Your Web browser is your gateway to the World Wide Web. A browser is the client software that allows you to access and view any document on the Web. There are a number of Web browsers that you can use to access the Web, and the number of choices available grows every month.

Even if you're an accomplished Web surfer, it's a good idea to keep up to date on the most popular browsers. Different Web browsers have different features, and they all display Web pages with slight variations. Older Web browsers, which are still in widespread use, often have trouble displaying some of the newer HTML3 features. If you're planning to create Web pages with HTML, you'll want to test them with a number of different Web browsers.

In this section, we'll take a look at Netscape, which is the most popular browser available today.

▶ **1** To navigate to a Web page, you can type in the URL for the page here.

6 Experiment with your Web browser to get an understanding of how navigation works on the World Wide Web. It's a good idea to use a few different browsers and note the differences. Knowing how users browse the Web is an important part of understanding how you should construct your own HTML pages.

TIP SHEET

▶ Not all browsers look alike. Read the documentation for your Web browser for specific details.

▶ New Web browsers are constantly being released, and existing ones are updated regularly. Make sure you're using the most recent version of your Web browser. You can usually find updates on the home page of your Web browser's publisher.

2 Use these directional buttons to navigate backward and forward through the list of documents you have recently accessed.

3 The button with the house on it always takes you back to your home page, no matter where you are. By default, most browsers set this button to display their home page, but you can specify the URL for your home page in the Options menu.

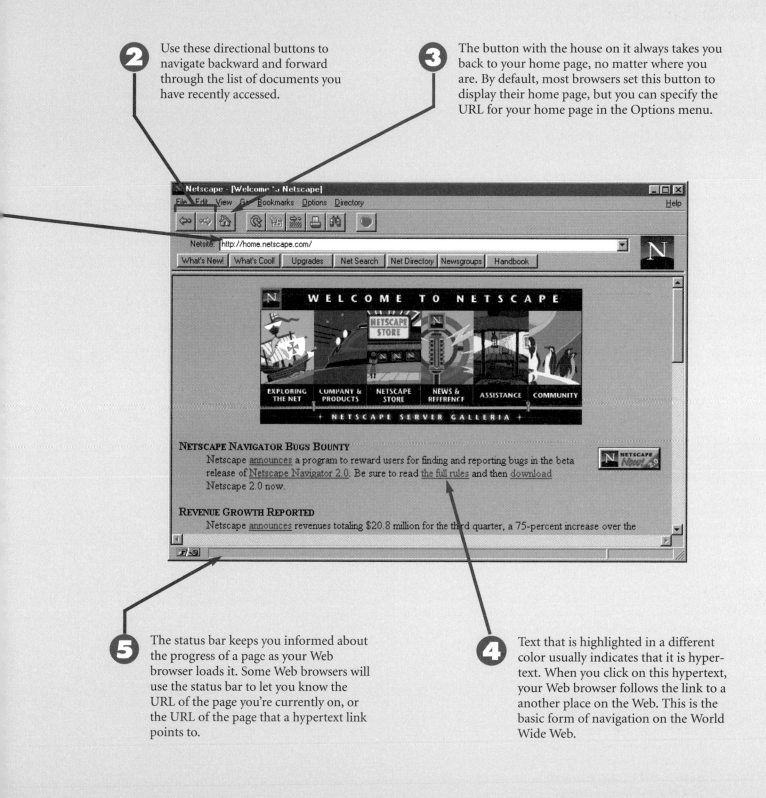

5 The status bar keeps you informed about the progress of a page as your Web browser loads it. Some Web browsers will use the status bar to let you know the URL of the page you're currently on, or the URL of the page that a hypertext link points to.

4 Text that is highlighted in a different color usually indicates that it is hypertext. When you click on this hypertext, your Web browser follows the link to a another place on the Web. This is the basic form of navigation on the World Wide Web.

How to Use a Hypertext Link

U sing a hypertext link to move from one place to another is one of the most common activities on the World Wide Web. In fact, hypertext links are the very essence of the Web. This lesson explains how to use a link and describes a little of what happens behind the scenes.

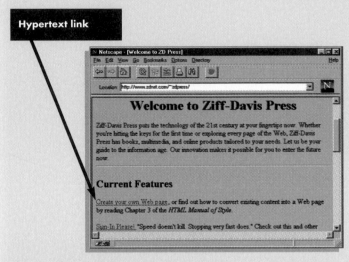

Hypertext link

To find a link on the page, look for text that's displayed in a different color. By default, hypertext links you haven't used are blue. Links you've already visited are purple. These colors can be changed, however.

Create your own Web page, or find out how to convert
Chapter 3 of the *HTML Manual of Style*.

2 Using your mouse, place the pointer over the hypertext link and click. There will be a brief delay after you press on the hypertext link.

3 During this delay, your browser client is contacting the Web server referenced in the hypertext link's URL. It is attempting to retrieve the referenced document.

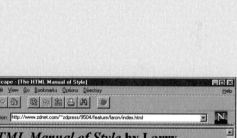

5 Not all links appear as text. Many links appear in images, such as buttons or icons. Sometimes a colored border will appear around the image, or it will be designed to look like a button. In many browsers, the cursor will change to a hand when it passes over a hypertext link. These visual clues help the reader understand that it is a link. However, sometimes there are no visual clues. Understanding the need to provide visual clues is an important part of being an HTML author.

4 Once the contact has been established, your browser begins displaying the new document.

CHAPTER 2

HTML and the Web

HTML isn't the only way to present information on the Web, but it's the glue that holds everything together. In addition to being a markup language for displaying text, images, and multimedia, HTML provides instructions to Web browsers in order to control how documents are viewed and how they relate to each other. For all its simplicity, HTML is a very powerful language.

In this chapter, we'll take a look at how HTML interacts with the Web, and we'll explore some of the ways that it's being used today on popular Web sites.

How HTML Works with the Web

Without HTML, the World Wide Web wouldn't exist. HTML allows the individual elements on the Web to be brought together and presented as a collection. Text, images, multimedia, and other files can all be packaged together using HTML. This section explains the basic principles behind the interaction between HTML and the World Wide Web.

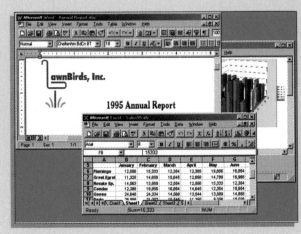

▶ **1** The author of the Web page assembles all of the materials necessary, including text, charts, images, and sounds.

TIP SHEET

▶ The speed of your Web browsing software largely depends on the type of Internet connection you have. Although a modem connection at 14.4Kbps is acceptable, you should consider upgrading your hardware and contacting an Internet Service Provider who can supply a faster connection. (See the Appendix for more information on Internet Service Providers.)

▶ You can always view the HTML source code for a particular page through your browser. Once you've mastered the basics of HTML, this is a great way to learn how other authors put together their HTML documents. To view the source code of the current document in Netscape, choose Document Source from the View menu.

2 All of the material for the Web page is linked together using HTML. HTML codes control the appearance, layout, and flow of the page. The amazing thing about HTML is that it is all done with simple text codes that anyone can understand.

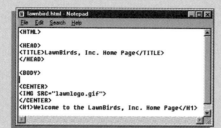

3 When someone connects to a Web server from his or her computer, the HTML file is transferred from server to client. Because an HTML file is simple text, this usually happens very quickly.

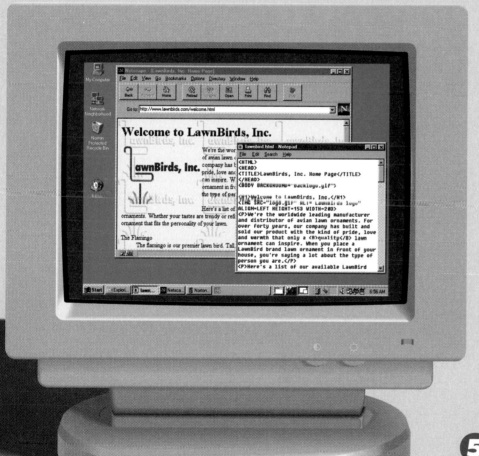

4 The Web browsing software (the client) interprets the layout and markup commands specified in the HTML file and then displays the text exactly as the HTML author intended.

5 Any images and charts on the page are retrieved as well. The HTML file tells the Web browser what images to download and how to display them on the page.

Six Cool Things You Can Do with HTML

There are many ways you can use HTML to publish content on the World Wide Web. Using this book, you'll learn the techniques you need to know to create timely, informative, and compelling HTML documents.

As you read this book and explore the Web on your own, you'll discover how the HTML pros created their Web pages. As you're sure to discover, there are a lot of cool things you can do with HTML. Here's just a small sample.

1 You can create a personal home page and leave your mark on the World Wide Web.

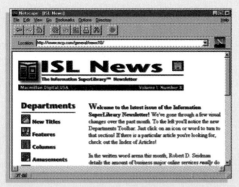

6 You can create a newsletter on the Web, with pictures and sounds. Using some of the advanced HTML tricks explained in this book, you can format the newsletter to give it a slick, professional appearance.

TIP SHEET

▶ **The best way to get ideas for your own Web pages is to explore the work of other HTML authors. After reading this book, you'll know how to interpret existing pages and borrow techniques from other authors.**

▶ **To keep an eye on the cutting edge, visit the Cool Site of the Day page at http://cool.infi.net/.**

2 You can create a page for your company to advertise and promote products and services.

3 You can build a catalog on the World Wide Web, complete with product descriptions and photographs. You can even incorporate fill-in order forms so that your customers can order products from you on line.

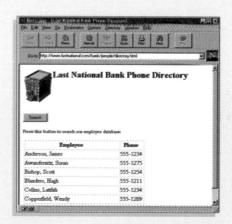

4 You can create a searchable phone directory for your company or organization.

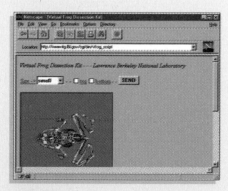

5 You can teach people how to dissect a frog.

CHAPTER 3

Getting Started with HTML

 By the time you finish reading this book, you'll be an expert HTML author. But along the way, there's a lot to learn. This chapter will introduce you to the basics of HTML—consider it HTML boot camp.

We'll take a quick look at Notepad, which is the only tool you really need to write HTML documents. We'll also go over the fundamentals of a basic HTML document. You'll even learn how to write your first Web page!

It might be tempting to skip ahead and check out the "cool stuff" in the later chapters of this book. But if you spend some time going over the basics, it will serve you well in the long run.

Enough chatter. Let's get going.

How to Use Notepad

HTML isn't really anything more than plain text. For that reason, you don't need any special editors or compilers to create HTML files. In fact, you can create all of your HTML files with the simplest of text editors. There are many specialized HTML editors and converters available, and you may decide to choose one of them based on your particular needs. But for all the HTML examples in this book, we'll use Windows Notepad to illustrate just how simple creating HTML can be.

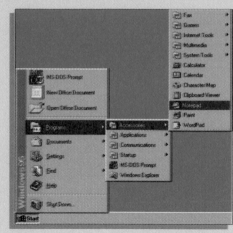

1 To open Notepad, click on the Start button in the lower-left corner of your screen. Then choose Programs, followed by Accessories. Click on the Notepad icon.

6 To save your HTML file, first pull down the File menu. If this is a new file that you started from scratch, choose Save As and then type a file name. Remember to use .htm or .html as the file extension. (Check with your Web server administrator to find out which extension you should use.) If this is an existing file that you opened from Notepad, you can just choose Save from the File menu.

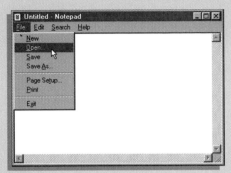

2 Notepad begins with a blank document. You can begin typing to create a new document. To open an existing text file from disk, pull down the File menu and choose Open.

3 Choose the file name from the Open File dialog box. Notepad's Open File dialog window normally only shows files with the extension .txt. You'll want to change the Files of Type selection to All Files if you're opening or saving an HTML file, which uses the extension .htm or .html.

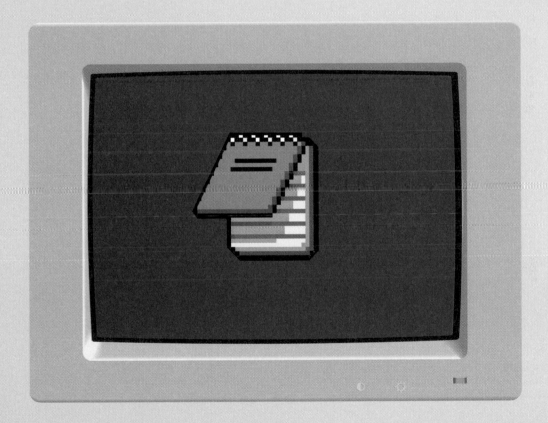

Editing text is easy using and keyboard. Position the then select text with your

Selected text

5 HTML files usually contain very long lines that will run off the edge of the page. Notepad has a feature called Word Wrap that will format these lines to fit entirely within the window, making them much easier to read. To activate this feature, pull down the Edit menu and select Word Wrap.

4 Once you've opened an existing file or begun typing a new one, you can easily edit your text. Notepad has all the basic editing functions of a word processor. For example, you can select blocks of text for cut and paste operations.

How to Use Markup Tags

The use of markup tags is what separates HTML from plain old text. Markup tags are used extensively in HTML, and they provide ways to control text formatting, create links to other documents, and even incorporate images and sounds. In short, markup tags are the key to making HTML pages work.

```
The pioneers ventured Westward in
hopes of blazing a trail of prosperity
in the bold new frontier.
```

 1 Open a new file in Notepad and type in the words **a bold new frontier**. In this example, we'll make this text appear in boldface type.

5 Almost every markup tag in HTML requires both a starting tag and an ending tag. One notable exception is the paragraph marker, <P>, which does not require an ending </P> tag.

TIP SHEET

▶ For a complete list of markup tags available in HTML 3.0, refer to the Appendix in this book.

▶ Markup tags are not case-sensitive. For example, the body element tag (which you'll learn about in the next lesson) can be typed as <BODY>, <body>, or even <BoDy>.

‹B›the bold new frontier.

2 HTML markup tags are easy to create. They consist of a left angle bracket, the name of the tag, and a right angle bracket. The left and right angle brackets are also known to some as *less-than* and *greater-than* symbols. To start a boldface markup tag, type **‹B›** where you'd like the boldface type to begin.

markup.html - Notepad

File   Edit   Search   Help

```
<HTML>
<B>
<TITLE>
<P>
<IMG>
<BODY>
<STRONG>
<I>
<ADDRESS>
<CENTER>
<TABLE>
```

Netscape - [The Story of the Pioneers]

File Edit View Go Bookmarks Options Directory   Help

Location: file:///C|/My Documents/How to Use HTML/HTML Files/pion

The pioneers ventured Westward in hopes of blazing a trail of prosperity in **the bold new frontier.**

new frontier ‹/B›

3 Locate the place where you'd like the boldface to stop. At this point, you need to create an ending tag for the boldface type. An ending tag looks just like a starting tag, except it is preceded by a forward slash character (/). To mark the end of the boldface tag, type **‹/B›**.

4 When viewed with a Web browser, the text between the ‹B› and ‹/B› tags will appear in boldface.

How to Write a Simple HTML Document

Now that you've learned how to create markup tags, the next step is to learn how to put them together to create a simple HTML Document.

The basic HTML document contains two parts: the *head* and the *body*. The head section contains important information about the document itself, such as the title. The actual text, images, and markup tags are placed in the body section. You'll learn the specifics of both sections in the next chapter.

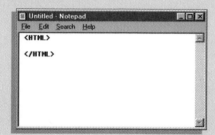

1 The first markup tag in every HTML document is the <HTML> tag. This lets Web browsers know that everything in the file is HTML text. Open a new blank document in Notepad. Type <**HTML**> on one line, and then on the next line, close the tag by typing <**/HTML**>. From now on, everything you type in this document should go between these two tags.

8 There it is—your first HTML document. It may not look like much at this point, but you should give yourself a pat on the back. You're now officially an HTML author. Congratulations!

7 Using your Web browser, open your new HTML document. Because your file is on your local desktop machine and not on the Web, you'll need to use the Open File option in your Web browser. With Netscape, choose Open File from the File menu, go to the folder where you saved your document, and select it.

6 Save your HTML file in Notepad with a descriptive file name, such as **first.htm**.

TIP SHEET

▶ **You might want to use this simple HTML document as a template for future documents you create. Instead of starting from scratch each time, you can open this document, replace the title and the text you used above, and save the file under a new name.**

▶ **Before you move on to the next page, take a moment to review everything you've learned so far. HTML is simple to use, but memorizing the basics will save you a lot of time and frustration.**

```
<HTML>

<HEAD>

</HEAD>

</HTML>
```

2 The head section comes next. Type <HEAD> on the line after the first HTML tag, followed by </HEAD> on the next line to create the section.

```
<TITLE>My First Web Page</TITLE>
</HEAD>

</HTML>
```

3 One of the key head elements is the title of your HTML document. To start the title tag, start a new line between the <HEAD> and </HEAD> tags and type <TITLE>. Now enter a title for your document, such as **My First Web Page**. Finally, end the title by typing </TITLE> on the same line.

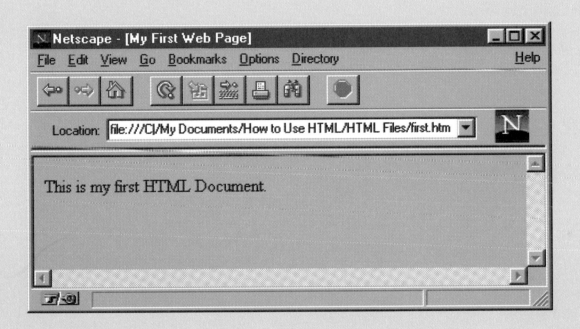

```
<BODY>
This is my first HTML Document.
</BODY>
```

5 Right now, your HTML document is properly formatted, but it doesn't have any content. Fortunately, that's simple enough to change. On a new line between the beginning and ending body tags, begin typing some text, such as **This is my first HTML document.**

```
<TITLE>My First Web Page</TITLE>
</HEAD>

<BODY>

</BODY>
```

4 The next section of your HTML document is the body. This section contains most of the elements of your document. To create the body section, type <BODY> on the next line. On the next line after that, type </BODY> to mark the end of the section. Most of your text and HTML codes will be placed between these two tags.

How to Use Special HTML Editing Software

Throughout this book, you'll learn to write HTML3 documents with the simplest of tools: a text editor. Creating HTML documents with a text editor is the best way to learn the language.

However, before you continue, you should know that there are a number of specialized HTML editing programs available. Some have graphical interfaces, others feature online help. All of them make creating HTML documents much easier. Once you've mastered the HTML basics, you may want to try out one of these programs. In this section, we'll show you what you should look for in an HTML editor.

TIP SHEET

▶ Many of the best HTML editors available on the Internet are shareware. Shareware is a type of software marketing that allows you to try the software before you purchase it. If you decide that you like the software and want to keep it, you pay the author directly, according to the documentation supplied with the program. If you don't like the program, simply delete it and forget it. Shareware is a great way to find a program that's right for your tastes.

▶ Even if your favorite HTML editor doesn't support the latest HTML tags and features, you can always add them later using Notepad. Because HTML files are plain text, you can work on your HTML documents with just about any editor you like.

▶ ❶ Make sure the HTML editing software has support for all the HTML3 features. If it doesn't, you won't be able to use all the cool HTML tricks you'll learn in this book.

❺ Many of the best HTML editors are available right on the World Wide Web as shareware. That means you can download them and try them out before buying them. There are plenty of places on the Web to find HTML editors. One of the best places to start looking is the HTML Editors section in the Yahoo directory. The full URL is http://www.yahoo.com/Computers_and_Internet/Internet/World_Wide_Web/HTML_Editors/

❹ Another feature to look for is HTML syntax checking. Editors with this capability can check your document for HTML errors. Some will even fix the errors for you automatically.

2 Look for toolbars and other features that make creating HTML easier. To create a markup tag, you can click on a button instead of typing it in.

3 Many WYSIWYG (What You See Is What You Get) HTML editors are now available. These allow you to see what your HTML document will look like as you're putting it together. This feature will save you the trouble of having to load your page with a Web browser every time you want to see how things are progressing.

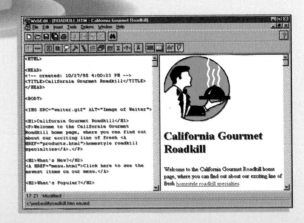

CHAPTER 4

Understanding the Basics of HTML

 Now that you've learned how to use markup tags and have even written your first HTML document, you're ready to dig a little deeper and learn the basics of the HTML language. In this chapter, you will uncover the different sections of an HTML document, such as the head and body, and learn what type of information goes in each. You'll also discover how to include basic paragraphs in your document, as well as insert headlines and special characters. So take a deep breath and get ready to dive right in.

How to Use the Head Section

In the previous chapter, you took a brief look at the <HEAD> section of an HTML document. This section of your HTML document is relatively small, but it conveys some very important information about your document to Web browsers and servers.

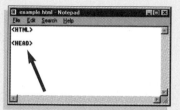

▶ **1** Open a new document in Notepad and type <HTML>. To begin the head section, insert an opening tag into your HTML document by typing <HEAD>.

▶ The title tag is used extensively by Web search engines; search engines use the text inside a title tag as a way to determine the actual contents of your page. So make sure your title is descriptive.

▶ Don't type any extra text in between the <HEAD> and </HEAD> tags. In most cases, the only line you'll insert between those two tags is your document title.

```
<HTML>

<HEAD>
<TITLE>HTML: Easier Than We Thought</TITLE>
</HEAD>
```

4 Close the head section by typing </HEAD> on the line below the title line.

The document title is displayed in the Web browser's title bar.

N Netscape - [HTML: Easier Than We Thought] _ □ ✕

2 The only element required in the head section is the Title of your document. Your title should be short enough to fit in the title bar of a typical browser window, but descriptive enough to explain what your HTML document contains.

```
<HTML>

<HEAD>
<TITLE>HTML: Easier Than We Thought</TITLE>
```

3 Insert a title tag within the head section by typing <**TITLE**>, followed by the actual title of your document. In this example, we'll name this document *HTML: Easier Than We Thought*. Go ahead and type in that title, then close the tag by typing </**TITLE**> on the same line.

How to Use the Body Section

The body section of your HTML document contains most of the text, graphics, hypertext links, and other information that will appear on the page. All of your HTML formatting tags, which describe the content and appearance of your document, are placed in the body section. These tags will be explained in detail in the next two chapters.

```
<HEAD>
<TITLE>HTML: Easier Than We Thought</TITLE>
</HEAD>

<BODY>  ←
```

 1 Insert the opening body tag by typing <BODY> on a new line in your document. Make sure that the new body tag follows the end of the head section of your document.

TIP SHEET

▶ You can use a number of enhancements to the <BODY> tag to control text colors and add background graphics to your HTML document. You'll learn these cool tricks in Chapter 9, "Advanced Graphics Techniques."

▶ Sometimes it's easier to type both the <BODY> and </BODY> tags on separate lines right away, and then fill in the rest of your HTML document between them.

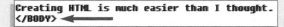

```
<BODY>
Creating HTML is much easier than I thought.
```

2 Following the <BODY> tag, begin entering the actual text of your HTML document. For this example, we'll just insert a simple sentence. Type **HTML is much easier than I thought.**

```
Creating HTML is much easier than I thought.
</BODY>
```

3 Close the body section of your document by typing </**BODY**> on a new line. Make sure that this closing tag appears before the </HTML> tag at the very bottom of your document.

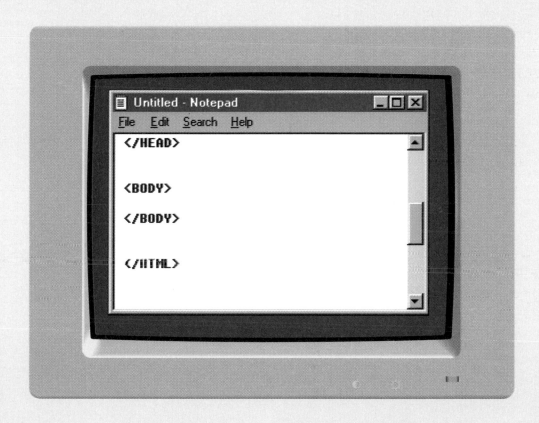

5 At this point, you should save your file in Notepad. Make sure you save it with an extension of .htm or.html (it doesn't matter which—all browsers will handle both types). Keep this file open, because you'll be adding to it in the next lesson.

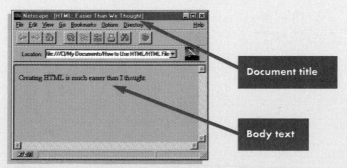

Document title

Body text

4 Here's what your HTML document looks like so far when viewed with Netscape. Notice the placement of the document title and the body text.

How to Use Headings

Headings are used in HTML documents to indicate different sections. There are six different Heading sizes, which range from very large to very small (smaller than the default body text). You should use headings judiciously, keeping them short and concise. The most common use for a heading is as the first line of a home page. In essence, it becomes a headline for your document.

▶ **1** To insert a heading into your document, place an opening tag anywhere in the body section. A heading tag follows the format of <H*x*>, where *x* is a number from 1 to 6, indicating the size from largest to smallest. To enter a level 1 heading, which is the largest, type <H1>.

TIP SHEET

▶ Headings are an excellent way to break up large amounts of text into smaller, digestible sections. But be careful not to overuse heading tags, or they'll make your document appear confusing.

▶ Think of heading tags as headlines. Generally, you'll only have one big headline for your document and a few smaller subheads to break the document into smaller sections.

▶ It's a good idea to repeat the document title as a Level 1 Heading at the very top of your page. This lets your readers know the title of the document without having to look at the title bar of their browsers.

▶ Headings can be compared in many ways to outlines. When structuring your documents with headings, use the same type of heading for elements of equal importance.

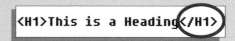

`<H1>This is a Heading`

2 Any text you enter immediately after the <H1> tag will be displayed in large bold type by a Web browser.

`<H1>This is a Heading</H1>`

3 Close the heading tag by typing </H1>.

4 You can experiment with different sized headings by changing the number of the heading tag to any value between 1 and 6. The result will look something like this.

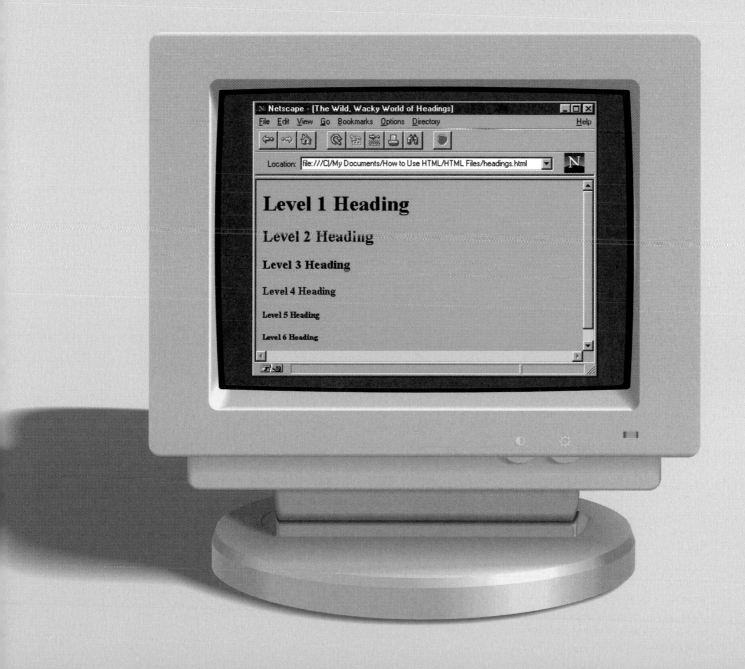

How to Use the Paragraph Tag

One of the most commonly used tags in HTML is the paragraph marker, which is used to break apart blocks of text into separate paragraphs. Any formatting that you perform in Notepad, such as placing carriage returns, extra spaces, or tab stops, will be ignored by Web browsers. The only way to indicate separate paragraphs is by using the paragraph marker. Unfortunately, despite its simplicity, the paragraph marker is also one of the most misunderstood tags in HTML.

▶ ❶ The most important thing to remember about the paragraph tag is that it marks the beginning of a paragraph, not the end. The original HTML standard used the paragraph marker differently, which has led to some confusion.

```
<P>This is a paragraph in HTML.</P>
<P>This is a second paragraph, only it's a
little bit longer. It still uses the same
opening and closing paragraph tags.</P>
<P>You can include all of the HTML character
formatting codes inside of paragraphs. For
example, you can make text appear <B>bold</B>
or in <I>italics</I>.</P>
```

❺ Continue entering new paragraphs of text, using the <P> tag to indicate the beginning of each.

```
paragraph.</P>
```

❹ You can indicate the end of a paragraph by typing </P>. However, this tag is optional. The end of the current paragraph is implied whenever a new paragraph marker is found by a browser.

TIP SHEET

▶ Rememember that in HTML3, paragraph tags are considered to be containers of text. That means each paragraph should have a starting <P> tag and an ending </P> tag. Early versions of HTML used the <P> tag as a paragraph separator.

▶ Paragraphs can contain more than plain text. You can place images, hyperlinks, and many other HTML elements inside paragraphs as well. You'll learn more about these elements in later chapters.

```
<BODY>

<P> ←

</BODY>
```

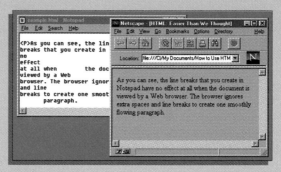

2 To insert a new paragraph, type <P> anywhere in the body section of your HTML document. This will tell the browser to insert a line space and start a new paragraph.

3 Enter the text of the paragraph after this tag. Remember that any carriage returns or line breaks you enter into Notepad will be ignored by a Web browser. The browser will continue to treat the text as part of the current paragraph until it sees another <P> tag.

How to Use Special Characters

By now, you may have noticed a potential problem with HTML. All of the markup tags are indicated by left and right angle brackets (greater-than and less-than symbols). These characters are reserved by HTML for use with tags. What happens when you want to include one of these characters in your text?

That's a good question, and the problem isn't limited to just those two symbols. A number of characters can't be typed directly into the body text HTML, including many foreign language symbols. Fortunately, HTML provides a solution through the use of *character entities*. By using special codes, HTML can display all of the characters in the ISO-Latin-1 (ISO 8859) character set. HTML3 also includes support for many mathematical symbols.

TIP SHEET

▶ **For a complete list of named and numbered character entities available, see the Appendix.**

▶ **One of the most commonly used special characters is the copyright symbol (©). Placing a copyright statement at the bottom of your Web document is a good idea and helps to remind your readers that your material may not be reproduced without your permission.**

▶ **Netscape also supports named character entities for the copyright and registered trademark symbols (© and ®). However, because these names are not standard HTML, not all browsers support them. Because the correct display of these symbols is important, it's a much better idea to use the numbered character entities for these symbols.**

```
<P>Goodbye, whispered Lauren. Then, without
another word, she walked out of Fabio's life
and went on to pursue her dream of becoming
a professional kazoo player.</P>
```

1 Locate your cursor at the position in the document where the character entity for the special character is to be placed.

```
&#174;
```

6 To insert a numerical character entity into HTML, type an ampersand, followed by a pound sign, the number of the character and a semicolon. For example, to enter the registered trademark symbol into your document, you would type ®. You can find a partial list of numerical character entities in the Appendix.

```
<P>&quot;Goodbye,&quot;| whispered Lauren.
Then, without another word, she walked out
of Fabio's life and went on to pursue her
dream of becoming a professional kazoo
player.</P>
```

2 A character entity begins with an ampersand (&), followed by the code, and ends with a semicolon. To place a double quote in your document, for example, type **"**.

3 Other common character entities for characters that are reserved for HTML tags are *<* for the less-than symbol; *>* for the greater-than symbol; and *&* for the ampersand. Note that these named character entities are case-sensitive.

über alles
mañana
resumé

4 You can also use named character entities for many foreign language symbols. For example, to create the umlaut used in the German phrase, *über alles*, you would type in **über alles**.

5 In addition to named character entities, you can use numbered character entities. HTML uses a subset of the ISO 8859/1 8-bit character set, and several characters, including the copyright symbol, trademark symbol, and mathematical symbols, are available when referenced by their numbered character entity.

CHAPTER 5

Formatting Text

 HTML was originally designed as a markup language, not as a formatting and layout specification. The key difference is that HTML allows the author to specify how certain elements are to be used, not necessarily how they're supposed to look. The actual details of presentation are left up to the client—the Web browser.

That's how HTML was originally designed, but that's not necessarily how things turned out. Increasingly, HTML designers are demanding greater control over the look and feel of their documents. HTML3 provides that control, and yet still allows HTML authors to take the first approach and allow formatting to be handled entirely by the browser.

As the author of your own document, you will decide how you want your page to look. In this chapter, you'll learn how to handle basic formatting for text and paragraphs. You'll also learn a few valuable techniques for breaking large amounts of text into readable chunks.

How to Format Characters with Physical Tags

HTML provides two general ways to apply formatting to text. The first group of formatting tags is collectively known as *physical markup tags.* This type of tag gets its name because it indicates a specific change in appearance. Bold and italic tags, for example, are known as physical markup tags because they directly specify how the text should appear on screen. In this section, we'll look at how you can use physical tags in HTML3.

▶ **1** In general, all character formatting tags work the same. Each has a starting tag and an ending tag. All of the text that falls between the two tags inherits the specified format. In addition, you can nest formatting tags inside one another to combine effects.

```
Superscript text appears <SUP>above</SUP>
Subscript text appears <SUB>below</SUB>
```

8 You can also format text as either superscript or subscript, which is text that appears slightly above or below the current line, respectively. Superscript and subscript numbers are often used in mathematical equations or to indicate footnotes. Using the ^{and} tags will mark text as superscript (slightly above the current line). _{and} will mark text as subscript (slightly below the current line).

```
<BIG>Big is not small,</BIG>
<SMALL>Small is not big.</SMALL>
```

7 You can change the font size of normal text. Using the <BIG> and </BIG> tags will increase the size of the indicated text relative to the default size. <SMALL> and </SMALL> will make the text smaller.

TIP SHEET

▶ Some formatting tags, especially the ones marked as new for HTML3, are not supported by all Web browsers. Use these tags only when absolutely necessary.

▶ When using superscript numbers to indicate footnotes, try adding the <SMALL> and </SMALL> tags to make the footnote numbers smaller than the normal text.

`<I>This is italic text</I>`

2 To create italic text, insert an <I> tag in the document, followed by a </I> tag. Any text between these two tags will be displayed in italics when viewed by a browser.

`<B>This is bold text.</B>`

3 To create bold text, insert <B> and </B> tags. Any text falling between these two tags will appear in boldface type.

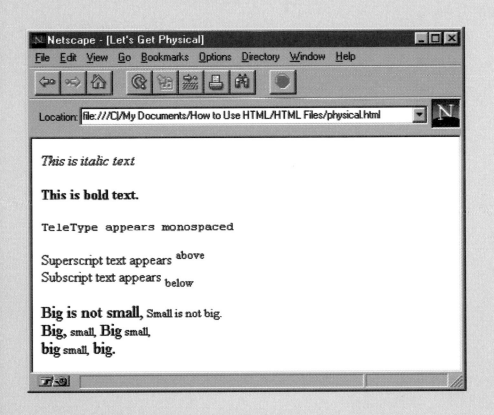

`<TT>TeleType appears monospaced</TT>`

4 To create text that is displayed in a monospaced font (such as Courier), use the <TT> and </TT> tags. Text falling between these two tags will be displayed in a fixed-width font, similar to the output from a teletype machine or typewriter.

`<S>Strike-through text</S>`

5 To create strike-through text, which is text with a single horizontal line running through it, use the <S> and </S> tags. This tag pair is new to HTML3.

`<U>Underlined Text</U>`

6 Underlined text can be displayed using the <U> and </U> tag pair. You should use these tags only when absolutely necessary, as underlined text is not widely supported by Web browsers.

How to Format Characters with Logical Markup Tags

On the previous page, you learned how to specify the appearance of text using physical markup tags. However, there is a second method for formatting text—through the use of *logical markup tags,* sometimes known as *information style elements.*

Logical tags take the approach that what's really important is the *type* of information being displayed, rather than exactly *how* it is displayed. Logical tags leave the actual appearance decisions—such as whether to display text in boldface, italics, or larger sizes—up to the browser (and ultimately the reader).

```
Say it with <EM>emphasis.</EM>
```

 1 When you want to add importance to a section of text, you can use the logical style tag called *emphasis.* Using the <EM> and </EM> tags will usually display the indicated text in italics. However, remember that with logical tags, the actual appearance of the text is determined by the end user's Web browser, not your HTML document.

```
The tag used to highlight a word or phrase that
will be defined is called the <DFN>defining
instance tag</DFN>.
```

 The <DFN> and </DFN> tags are used to highlight the *defining instance* of a term. This is a word or phrase that is being defined in the context of the paragraph in which it appears. This logical tag pair is new to HTML 3.0, and may not be supported by all browsers.

```
Say it with <STRONG>strong emphasis.</STRONG>
```

2 If a particular section of text is very important, you can mark it with *strong emphasis* by using the <STRONG> and </STRONG> tag pair. Most browsers tend to display strongly emphasized text in boldface.

```
<CODE>
var
  count : integer;
begin
  for count := 1 to 100 do
    begin
      smudgie := smudgie + 1
    end
end;
<CODE>
```

3 The <CODE> and </CODE> tags indicate that the text is to be presented as an example of *programming code*. In most browsers, this text will be displayed in a monospaced font, such as Courier. The <CODE> tags are used extensively in interactive computer manuals.

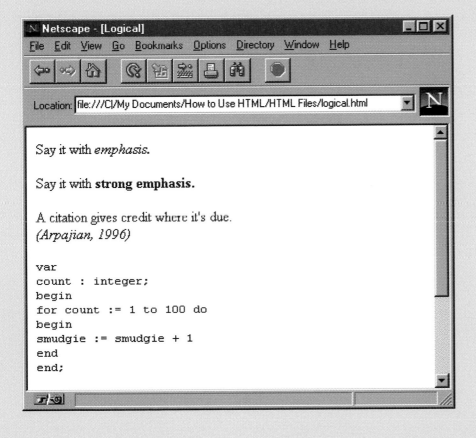

4 The <SAMP> and </SAMP> tags are very similar to the <CODE> tags, and are used to indicate sample text that isn't specifically programming code. Most Web browsers will handle both sets of tags in the same way.

```
The user types in <KBF>keyboard text</KBD>.
```

5 The <KBD> and </KBD> tags indicate text that is supposed to be typed in by the reader. By default, most browsers will display this text in a similar fashion to the <CODE> and <SAMP> tags.

```
A citation gives credit where it's due.
<CITE>(Arpajian, 1996)</CITE>
```

6 The <CITE> and </CITE> tags are used to insert a citation to give credit for a short quotation in the body of the document. Citations are typically displayed in italics.

Continue to next page ▶

How to Format Characters with Logical Markup Tags (Continued)

`<Q>This is a quote,</Q> she said.`

▶ **1** The <Q> and </Q> tags are used to offset a short quotation. This logical tag pair is new to HTML3.

▶ **Choosing when to use logical tags instead of physical tags can be difficult. A good rule is when you want to concentrate on the type of information being displayed, use logical tags; when you want to concentrate on the appearance, use physical tags.**

▶ **You can use both physical and logical tags together in the same document.**

```
The author of the book was <AUTHOR>L. Frank
Baum.</AUTHOR>
```

2 The name of the author of a document can be highlighted using the <AU> and </AU> tags. This tag pair is also new to HTML3.

```
<PERSON>James Polk</PERSON> is one of the least
remembered Presidents of the United States.
```

3 The **<PERSON>** and **</PERSON>** tags are used to highlight names of individuals. The **<PERSON>** element has a dual purpose: In addition to formatting the text, it allows the names to be recognized and extracted by indexing programs on the server. This tag pair is new to HTML3.

```
The official abbreviation for the word
abbreviation is <ABBREV>abbr.</ABBREV>, as
decided by <ACRONYM>ICOA</ACRONYM>,the
International Committee on Abbreviations.
```

```
<INS>This text has been inserted.</INS>
<DEL>This text has been deleted.</DEL>
```

5 The **<INS>** and **</INS>** tags are used to indicate text that has been added to a document. Likewise, the **<DEL>** and **</DEL>** tags indicate text that has been deleted. These tag pairs, which are also new to HTML3, are most often used in legal briefs or other documents where it is necessary to show both the original text and the alterations.

4 The **<ABBREV>** and **</ABBREV>** tags are used to indicate abbreviations. Likewise, the **<ACRONYM>** and **</ACRONYM>** pair are used to mark up acronyms. Both of these tag pairs are new to HTML3.

How to Format Paragraphs

Now that you've learned all the ways to format individual characters, words, and phrases, you're ready to examine the options you have for presenting entire sections of text. As with normal documents, the basic section of text in HTML is the paragraph. HTML3 provides many new ways to present, format, and align paragraphs.

1 The basic paragraph tag is always used to start a new paragraph. To indicate a paragraph, type <P>. This tells the Web browser to insert a line space and begin a new paragraph. The <P> tag always creates a simple, left-justified paragraph.

`<P>`

`<P ALIGN=CENTER NOWRAP>`

6 To combine formatting commands in the same paragraph, type all the attributes together in the same <P> tag. For example, to create a center-aligned paragraph with no word wrapping, type **<P ALIGN=CENTER NOWRAP>**.

Normally, text wraps around a figure.

Using the **CLEAR=LEFT** attribute forces the paragraph to wait until the margin is empty.

This paragraph contains no special formatting. As a result, it wraps around the image to the left. It will continue to flow along the side of the image until it reaches the bottom.

This paragraph was created using the <P CLEAR=LEFT> tag. It causes the Web browser to wait to start the paragraph until the left margin is clear.

5 Normally, paragraphs will wrap around an object in the margin, such as a figure or table. To force the paragraph to begin below the object, you can use the *CLEAR* attribute. Typing **<P CLEAR=LEFT>** moves the paragraph down until the left margin is clear. **CLEAR=RIGHT** forces the paragraph down to a point where the right margin is clear. **CLEAR=ALL** forces the paragraph to wait until both margins are clear.

`<P ALIGN=RIGHT>`

2 You can change the justification of the paragraph with the *ALIGN* attribute. To change the alignment of a paragraph, put the ALIGN statement in the paragraph tag, followed by the type of justification you want. To create a right-justified paragraph, type <**P ALIGN=RIGHT**>.

`<P ALIGN=CENTER>`

3 To create a centered paragraph, type <**P ALIGN=CENTER**>. To create a paragraph that is justified on both sides, type <**P ALIGN=JUSTIFY**>. You can also create a left-justified paragraph by typing <**P ALIGN=LEFT**>. However, since this is the default, just typing <**P**> will have the same effect.

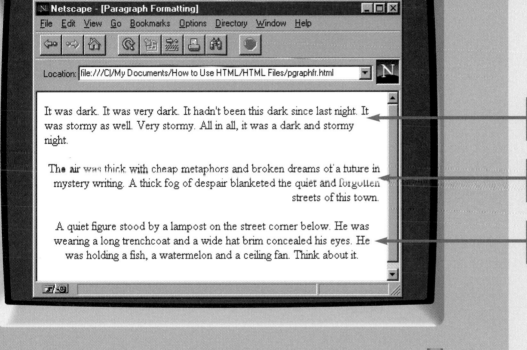

This paragraph is left-justified.

This paragraph is right-justified.

This paragraph is centered.

`<P NOWRAP>`

4 By default, the Web browser will wrap lines of text to keep the entire paragraph in view. You have the option of turning off word wrapping by including the *NOWRAP* command in the paragraph tag. To turn off word wrapping in a paragraph, type <**P NOWRAP**>. This will allow you to explicitly place line breaks using the <BR> tag, which is explained in the next section.

How to Use Text Breaks

Not all text fits neatly into paragraphs. Sometimes you want the reader's Web browser to end a line of text at a specific point. If you're using HTML to display poetry, lyrics, instructional materials, or any other type of information where specific formatting is necessary, you'll want to have control over the flow of text in the document.

```
<P>A partridge in a pear tree<BR>
```

▶ **1** To insert a line break at a specific point, type <BR>. This instructs the Web browser to immediately end the current line and begin placing text on the next line. A line break does not start a new paragraph.

```
<BLOCKQUOTE>
The <I>Twelve Days of Christmas</I> has
always been one of my favorite holiday
songs. It brings a sense of joyous
celebration,  especially when sung by a
group of friends.
</BLOCKQUOTE>
```

 4 To place an entire section of text apart from the rest, use the <BLOCKQUOTE> and </BLOCKQUOTE> tag pair. This tag, used in place of a paragraph tag, will offset an entire paragraph from the main body of text, usually by indenting it and adding extra spaces to the top and bottom. It is commonly used to highlight long quotations and passages.

```
Four calling birds<BR>
Five golden rings<BR>
Six geese a-laying<BR>
Seven swans a-swimming<BR>
Eight maids a-milking<BR>
```

2 You can use multiple line breaks to create a short, informal list of items. By creating a new paragraph before and after the list, you can separate it from the rest of your text.

3 Sometimes you'll want to visually break apart sections of text using a visible line. HTML supports this through the use of *horizontal rules*. These can be added anywhere in the document by typing <**HR**>. A thin line stretching across the entire window will be placed at that point in the text. Horizontal rules, like paragraphs, support the clear attribute to allow you to begin the line when the margins are clear.

`<HR>`

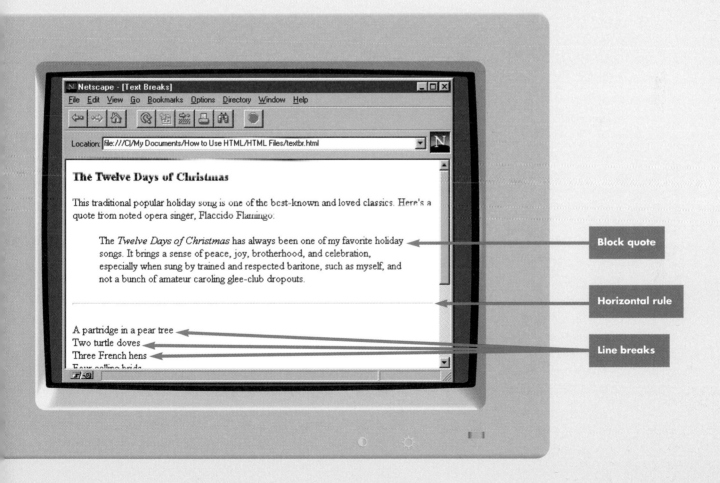

Block quote

Horizontal rule

Line breaks

How to Use Preformatted Text

Preformatted text allows you break away from the normal rules of HTML and quickly specify exactly how a section of text will appear in the reader's Web browser. When you're using preformatted text, you don't need to use the HTML markup tags—the text will appear exactly as you've typed it, complete with spaces, line breaks, and empty lines. Preformatted text is always displayed in a monospaced, fixed-width font.

1 To begin a section of preformatted text, type <PRE>.

Preformatted text can have character styles applied, such as bold and italic.

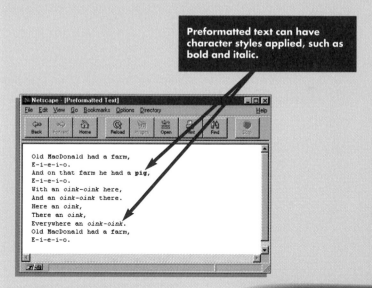

4 You can apply character formatting styles, such as bold and italic, in preformatted text. Headings and paragraphs will not work in preformatted text blocks, however.

TIP SHEET

▶ Preformatted text is a great way to create a quick and dirty table of data, such as names and phone numbers. However, HTML3 has full table support, and in most cases you'll want to use real tables whenever possible.

▶ Another good use for the <PRE> and </PRE> tags is to display samples of Internet e-mail or newsgroup posts in your HTML document. These messages often have specific layouts that are difficult to reproduce in straight HTML. Just cut and paste the original message into Notepad and then place the <PRE> and </PRE> tags at the beginning and end, respectively.

2 Now type the section of text exactly how you want it to appear. It's a good idea to limit the length of your lines to 65 characters or less, so that you can accommodate the screen width of most browsers. (Remember that browsers will not word wrap preformatted text.)

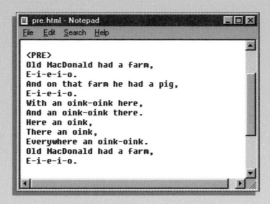

</PRE>

3 When you're finished entering your preformatted text, type </PRE> to mark the end of the section.

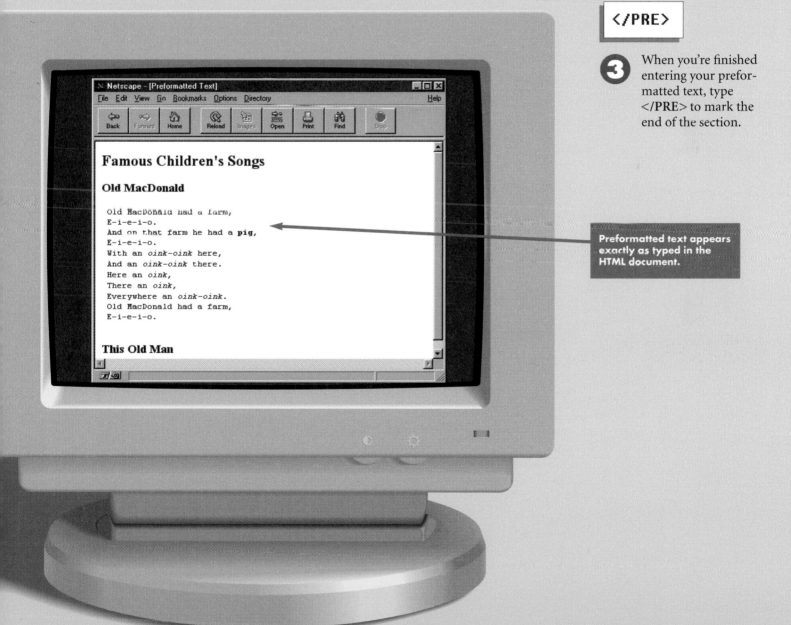

Preformatted text appears exactly as typed in the HTML document.

TRY IT!

Here is an opportunity to put the skills you've learned to work. You've been asked to create an informational HTML document for a company called LawnBirds, Inc. The company wants to create a simple home page on the Web that will tell customers something about their products.

You'll create the document from scratch using Notepad, and finish with a complete, working Web page.

Launch Notepad.

Turn Word Wrap on by selecting Word Wrap from the Edit menu.

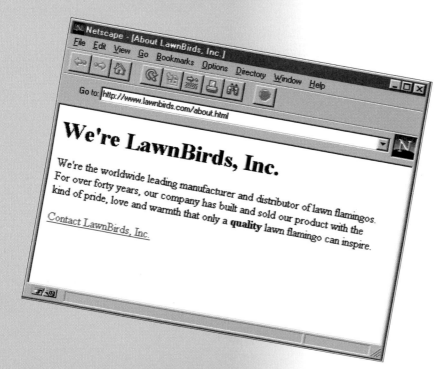

3

Type
\<HTML\> in
the blank
Notepad doc-
ument, and
then press
Enter.

4

Type
\<HEAD\>,
and then
press Enter.

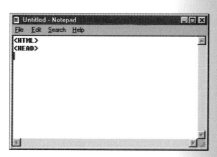

5

Type
\<TITLE\>, followed by the title of the
document, **About Lawnbirds, Inc.**

```
<HTML>
<HEAD>
<TITLE>About LawnBirds, Inc.
```

6

Type \</TITLE\> on the same line, and
then press Enter.

```
<TITLE>About LawnBirds, Inc.</TITLE>
```

7

Type \</HEAD\> to close the head section, and then press Enter.

```
<TITLE>About LawnBirds, Inc.</TITLE>
</HEAD>
```

8

Type
\<BODY\>, and then press Enter to start
the body section.

```
<TITLE>About LawnBirds, Inc.</TITLE>
</HEAD>
<BODY>
```

9

To create a
headline for
your page, type \<H1\>.

```
<TITLE>About LawnBirds, Inc.</TITLE>
</HEAD>
<BODY>
<H1>
```

10

On the same
line, type
**We're
LawnBirds,
Inc.**

11

Type \</H1\>,
and press Enter.

```
</HEAD>
<BODY>
<H1>We're LawnBirds, Inc.</H1>
```

Continue to next page ▶

TRY IT!

Continue
below

12

```
</HEAD>
<BODY>
<H1>We're LawnBirds, Inc.</H1>
<P>|
```

To start the
first paragraph, type <P>.

13

```
Untitled - Notepad
File  Edit  Search  Help
<HTML>
<HEAD>
<TITLE>About LawnBirds, Inc.</TITLE>
</HEAD>
<BODY>
<H1>We're LawnBirds, Inc.</H1>
<P>We're the worldwide leading
manufacturer and distributor of lawn
flamingos. For over forty years, our
company has built and sold our product
with the kind of pride, love and
warmth that only a quality lawn flamingo can
inspire.</P>
|
```

Type the
entire first
paragraph as
shown on the
screen.
Remember,
you do not
need to press Enter to start new lines of
text. At the end of the paragraph, type
</P> and press Enter.

14

```
warmth that only a <B>quality lawn flamingo
can inspire.</P>
```

The LawnBirds corporation is very
concerned with quality, and wants to
highlight that aspect of their business.
To make the word *quality* stand out in
the first paragraph, place the cursor
immediately before the word and type
<B>.

15

```
warmth that only a <B>quality</B>| lawn
flamingo can inspire.</P>
```

Immediately after the word *quality* type
</B>.

16

```
warmth that only a <B>quality</B> lawn
flamingo can inspire.</P>
<P>|
```

Start a new paragraph at the bottom of
the document by typing <P>.

17

```
warmth that only a <B>quality</B> lawn
flamingo can inspire.</P>
<P>Contact LawnBirds, Inc.|
```

Type **Contact LawnBirds, Inc.**

18

```
flamingo can inspire.</P>
<P>Contact LawnBirds, Inc.</P>|
```

Close the new paragraph by typing
</P> on the same line.

```
flamingo can inspire.</P>
<P><A HREF="contact.html">Contact LawnBirds,
```

Let's make this last sentence a hyperlink that points to another document with contact information. Position the cursor before the word *Contact* and type **<A HREF="contact.html">**. (You'll create the actual contact information document later.)

```
<P><A HREF="contact.html">Contact LawnBirds,
Inc.</A></P>
```

Position the cursor after the word *Inc.* in the second paragraph and type **</A>** to close the hyperlink tag.

```
<P><A HREF="contact.html">Contact LawnBirds,
Inc.</A></P>
</BODY>
```

Type **</BODY>** on the line below the last paragraph to end the body section. Then press Enter.

```
<P><A HREF="contact.html">Contact LawnBirds,
Inc.</A></P>
</BODY>
</HTML>
```

Type **</HTML>** to mark the end of the document.

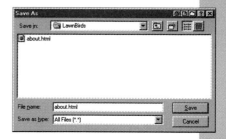

Save the file in Notepad, naming it **about.html**.

Load the new HTML document using the Open File option in the File menu of your Web browser.

CHAPTER 6

Using Hypertext Links

The single greatest feature of the World Wide Web is its diverse collection of documents, which number in the millions. All of these documents are brought together through the use of hypertext links. Users navigate the Web by clicking on the links that HTML authors provide. Hypertext links are a crucial part of HTML—which, after all, is short for *Hypertext Markup Language.*

In this chapter, we'll look at the simple process behind how hyperlinks work in your HTML documents. You'll also learn how to link to a specific point in a large document by using the ID attribute. Finally, we'll take a look at the difference between using absolute and relative path names in your hyperlink references.

Linking is one of the easiest and most important parts of using HTML. So warm up your Web browser and Notepad and get ready to explore.

How to Create a Hyperlink

Hyperlinks connect two different documents. You can link to one of your own documents or to any other document on the World Wide Web. You can even link to a different section in the same document. It is very easy to create links with HTML, and you only need to follow a few simple steps.

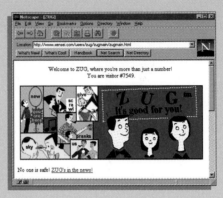

▶ **1** Use your Web browser to locate the document you want to link. You can link to any other document on the World Wide Web.

6 Once you've created your link, check to make sure it works by clicking on it while using your Web browser. Note that by default, most Web browsers display hypertext links as underlined text in a different color than normal text. This lets your readers know that clicking on the text will take them to another document.

```
/zugmain.html">the Zug Home Page.</A>
```

5 Finish the anchor tag by typing </A> on the same line.

```
/zugmain.html">the Zug Home Page.
```

4 Type some descriptive text (also known as the *link text*) after the anchor tag to let readers know something about where this link will take them.

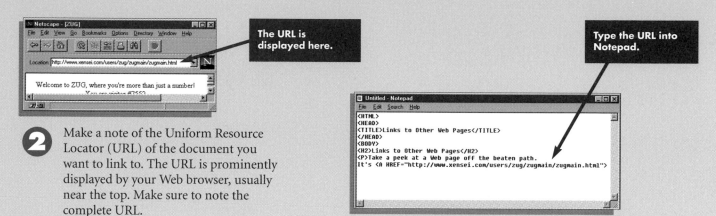

The URL is displayed here.

Type the URL into Notepad.

2 Make a note of the Uniform Resource Locator (URL) of the document you want to link to. The URL is prominently displayed by your Web browser, usually near the top. Make sure to note the complete URL.

3 To make a link to another document, you need to use a special type of HTML tag known as an *anchor tag*, also commonly known as a *link tag*. Locate the place in your HTML document where you want to insert the hypertext link. Type <A HREF=", followed by the URL of the document you want to link to. Then close the tag by typing ">.

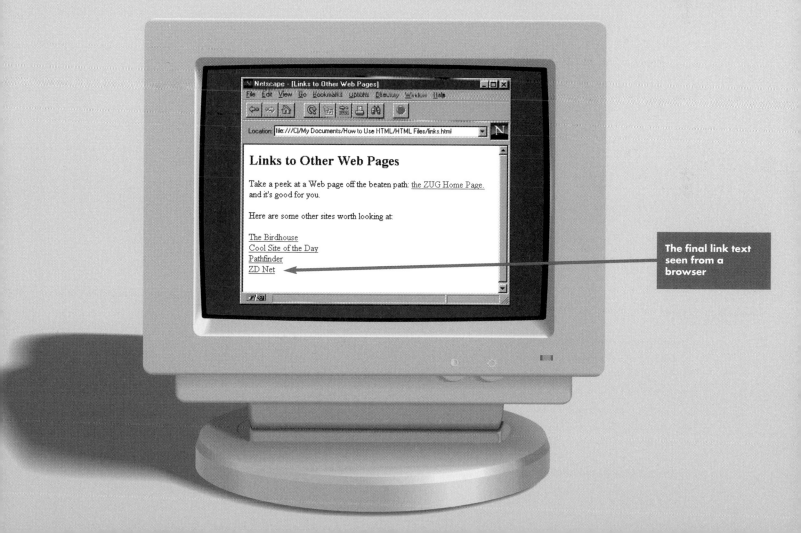

The final link text seen from a browser

How to Use the ID Attribute

When you create a simple link to a Web page using the technique you learned on the previous page, the reader is always taken to the top of the new page. What if you want to link to a particular section of a document and take the reader immediately to that point? The new HTML3 ID attribute is the answer.

Assigning an ID to an element in your HTML document allows hyperlinks to point directly to that element instead of to the very top of the page. You can use the ID attribute for most HTML elements, such as paragraphs, headings, and lists.

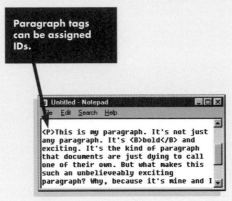

Paragraph tags can be assigned IDs.

1 Locate the element you'd like to name with an ID. This can be almost any element in your document, but it is usually a paragraph or heading.

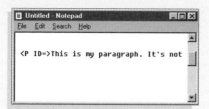

2 Inside the element's opening tag, just after the letter P, insert a space and type **ID=**.

3 Your element ID needs a name. The hyperlinks will use this name to take readers directly to this section of your document. In this example, we'll simply name the element "MyParagraph".

4 Type the name of your ID, inside quotation marks.

5 To create a hyperlink directly to this element, add a pound sign and the ID name inside your hyperlink tag. For example, to link directly to "MyParagraph", a typical hyperlink might look like the one above.

How to Use Relative Path Names

In the beginning of this chapter, you learned how to create a hyperlink by pointing to the full URL of another document. However, if you're linking to different documents on the same Web server (usually your own), you don't always need to use the full URL. You can use *relative path names.*

Web browsers, even when running on PC or Macintosh machines, always follow UNIX style path names. This means that directories (folders) are separated by forward slash marks (/), and higher-level directories are indicated by two periods (..).

```
<A HREF="newfile.html">
```

1 The simplest relative path name is no path name at all. If you're linking to another document that's in the same directory, all you have to do is type in the file name of the new document in place of the full URL. For example, to link to a document named newfile.html, type <AHREF="newfile.html">.

TIP SHEET

▶ Remember that in UNIX, file names are case-sensitive. To keep things simple, it's a good idea to always name your files in lowercase letters.

▶ Don't forget that UNIX systems use a forward slash (/) for path names, not the backward slash that DOS users are familiar with.

```
<A HREF="budget96/budget.html">
```

2 To link to documents or files in a sub-directory, all you need to specify is the path and file name relative to the current document. For example, to link to a document called budget.html in a subdirectory named budget96, you would type <A HREF="budget96/budget.html">.

```
<A HREF="../main.html">
```

3 You can also navigate up the directory tree of your server by using two periods (..) to move up one level. For example, to link from the budget.html file in the previous example back to the main document, you would type <A HREF="../main.html">.

```
<A HREF="../../main.html">
```

4 If the new document was two levels above the current one, you would separate each level with a slash, and type <A HREF="../../main.html">.

5 The single greatest advantage to using relative path names is portability. If you do your HTML development on a local machine, and then up-load your finished work to a Web server, you can save yourself the trouble of having to reset all of your hyperlinks to reflect the new location. Likewise, relative path names will save you the headache of changing your hyperlinks if you move your existing HTML files to an entirely new Web server.

CHAPTER 7

Creating Lists in HTML

 Everyone makes lists. Whether you use them for groceries, to-do items, or holiday gifts and cards, lists are an important part of your life.

Lists are also important on the World Wide Web. The environment of the Web calls for information to be presented in a concise and timely manner. Lists are ideal vehicles for delivering all kinds of information on line.

As an HTML author, you have many choices for how to create and present lists. In this chapter, we'll look at ways to create *unordered lists*, *ordered* (numbered) *lists*, and a special type of list known as a *definition list*. You'll also learn how to combine multiple levels of lists.

How to Create Unordered Lists

The simplest list in HTML is the unordered, or bulleted, list. This is ideal for listing items that have no particular hierarchy or order of importance. Unordered lists are very common on the Web and are used to convey items of note in a quick and concise manner. Web browsers usually place bullets or other markers in front of each item in an unordered list.

1 Locate the part of your HTML document where you want to insert a list.

```
<LI>Potatoes
</UL>
```

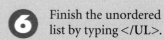

6 Finish the unordered list by typing </UL>.

```
<UL>
```

2 Begin the unordered list by typing <UL>, and then press Enter. The *<UL>* tag tells the Web browser to treat this section of text as an unordered list. Unordered lists will usually be indented from the main document and list items will be formatted with bullets. The size and type of bullets used are determined by the Web browser.

```
<UL>
<LH>My Grocery List</LH>
```

3 Create a heading for your list. This is an optional brief description of what your list contains. To create a list header, type **<LH>**, followed by a brief summary of the list contents. Then type **</LH>** to close the list heading tag. For example, to create a list heading for a grocery list, you would type **<LH>My Grocery List</LH>**.

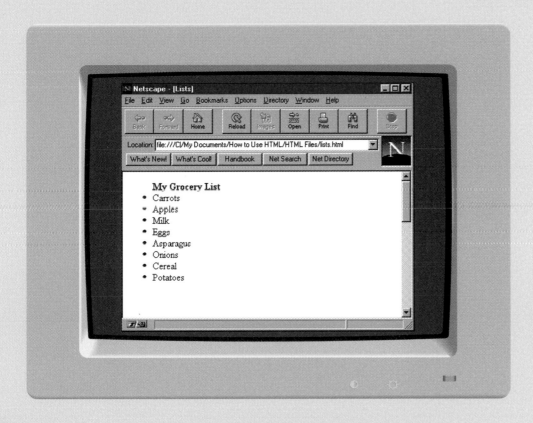

5 Continue typing **<LI>** followed by text for each item in your list. Press Enter after each item.

```
<UL>
<LH>My Grocery List</LH>

<LI>Carrots
```

4 To create the first item in your list, type **<LI>**. Then type the text of the item itself. *<LI>* is an open tag, which means that you do not need to type </LI> at the end of each item.

How to Create Ordered Lists

S ometimes you need to list items in a specific order. Examples of this type of list include step-by-step instructions and "Top 10" lists. HTML provides a way to do this through ordered lists. Web browsers will place a number in front of each item, increasing the number by one for each entry down the list.

‹OL›

▶ **1** To create an ordered list, locate the place in your document where you'd like to begin the list and type ‹OL›.

‹/OL›

7 Type ‹/OL› to close the ordered list.

`<LH>How to Ride a Bicycle</LH>`

2 To create an optional heading for the ordered list, type <LH> followed by the heading. Then close the heading tag by typing </LH>.

`<LI>Fasten your safety helmet in place.`

3 To enter the first item of your list, type <LI> followed by the item. There is no need to include a closing </LI> tag.

`<OL SEQNUM=57>`

4 To start the sequence of your list at a number other than 1, you can use the *SEQNUM* attribute inside the <OL> tag. For example, to start an ordered list at number 57, type <OL SEQNUM=57>.

`<OL CONTINUE>`

5 You can start the numbering sequence of an ordered list at the spot where the last list on the page left off. Type <OL CONTINUE> to force the ordered list to start with the next number in sequence from the previous list.

`<LI SKIP=5>`

6 You can skip numbers in your ordered list by including the *SKIP* attribute inside the list item tag. For example, to skip five numbers between steps, type <LI SKIP=5> when starting the new item.

How to Create Definition Lists

Definition lists are different from other lists in HTML, because each item in a definition list contains two parts: a term and a definition. Definition lists are typically used for glossaries and dictionaries. With a little creativity, however, they can be put to use in many different ways, such as product catalogs and even poetry.

`<DL>`

1 To create a definition list in your HTML document, type <DL> at the point where you'd like the list to begin.

`</DL>`

7 Type </DL> to close your definition list.

6 As with ordered and unordered lists, there are no closing tags for list items. Therefore, it is not necessary to type </DT> or </DD> at the end of your terms and definitions.

`<LH>Guide to Fruits and Berries</LH>`

2 To create an optional list header, type <LH> followed by some text that describes the contents of the list. Close the list header tag by typing </LH>.

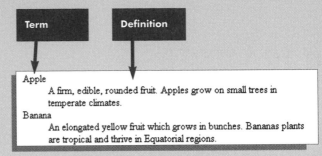

Apple
    A firm, edible, rounded fruit. Apples grow on small trees in
    temperate climates.
Banana
    An elongated yellow fruit which grows in bunches. Bananas plants
    are tropical and thrive in Equatorial regions.

3 As mentioned earlier, definition lists are slightly different from ordered and unordered lists. Each item in a definition list is made up of two separate parts: the *term* and the *definition*. Typically, browsers will display the term on one line and the definition indented on the next line.

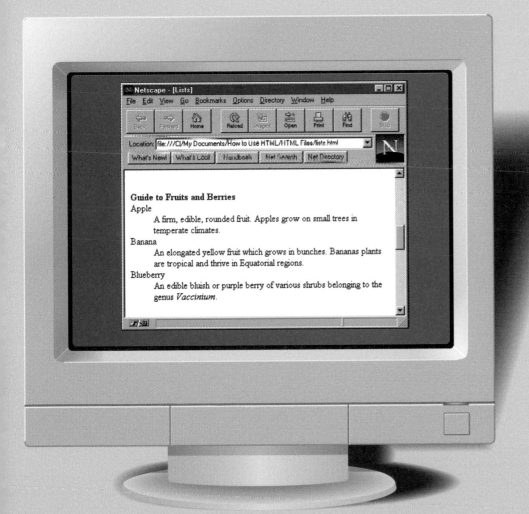

`<DT>Apple`

4 To create a definition term, type <DT> followed by text describing the element being defined. For example, to begin a definition of the word *apple*, you would type <DT>Apple.

`<DD>A firm, edible, rounded fruit.`
`    Apples grow on small trees in`
`    temperate climates.`

5 To create the definition, type <DD>, followed by the text of the definition. For example, to create a definition for the term in the previous step, you would type <DD>a firm, edible, rounded fruit.

How to Create Lists within Lists

In the beginning of this chapter, we learned that lists are extremely flexible and powerful tools in HTML. Sometimes you'll want to create lists within lists, especially when you need to create a hierarchy of items, such as in outlines or detailed instructions. Creating lists within lists is easy in HTML.

`<OL>`

▶ **1** Begin the first list by typing <OL>. In this example, we're assuming that the first list is an ordered list, but in reality, it can be any type of list you want.

`</OL>`

5 Enter the remaining items in the original list. Then press Enter and type </OL> when you're finished.

TIP SHEET

▶ It helps to keep your lists and list items indented in Notepad. Even though Web browsers will ignore the extra spaces, keeping everything organized this way will help you keep a handle on your HTML code.

▶ You can nest lists as many levels deep as you like. However, it's good practice to limit your nesting to three levels or less in order to make sure that the lists stay within the visible area of the reader's Web browser.

```
<OL>
  <LI>Remove your LawnBird Flamingo
      from its attractive box.
  <LI>Assemble your tools. You'll
      need the following:
```

2 Enter your list items one by one, beginning each item with <LI>.

```
<OL>
  <LI>Remove your LawnBird Flamingo
      from its attractive box.
  <LI>Assemble your tools. You'll
      need the following:
      <UL>  ←
```

3 When you reach a step that requires a nested list, begin another list. The Web browser will automatically format this new list to fall underneath the current item in the first list. For example, to create a nested list under Step 2 in your original list, just type <UL>.

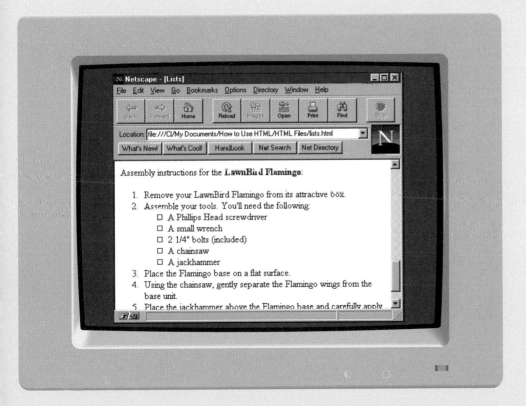

4 Start entering items in your new list. When you're finished, close the new list by typing </UL>. You must close the new list before continuing to enter items in the original list.

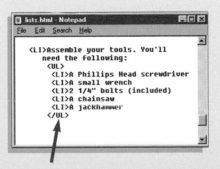

```
<LI>Assemble your tools. You'll
    need the following:
    <UL>
      <LI>A Phillips Head screwdriver
      <LI>A small wrench
      <LI>2 1/4" bolts (included)
      <LI>A chainsaw
      <LI>A jackhammer
    </UL>
```

CHAPTER 8

Adding Graphics to HTML

 In the early days of the World Wide Web, graphics were considered to be little more than novelties—a cheap trick to spice up a Web page. But today, graphical images are an integral part of any HTML document. You'd be hard-pressed to find a popular site on the Web that didn't use images extensively.

Knowing how to include graphics in HTML, and more important, knowing how to use graphics correctly, is a crucial part of putting together a Web page. Good HTML documents don't just show images, they integrate them and use them effectively.

In this chapter, we'll look at the types of images used on the Web, and show you how to use HTML to include them in your Web pages. You'll also discover secrets for formatting your images for maximum visibility and effectiveness.

What Are GIF and JPEG Files?

The two most common image file formats in use on the World Wide Web are GIF (.GIF) and JPEG (.JPG) files. The GIF format is directly supported by every graphical Web browser, while JPEG is still gaining acceptance as a standard image format on the World Wide Web. Although both GIF and JPEG files can be used in your HTML documents, there are a few important differences between the two formats.

▶ ❶ The GIF format, developed by CompuServe, is a cross-platform format, which means it can be viewed on almost any type of computer system, making it ideal for use on the World Wide Web. The one significant limitation of the GIF format is that images are limited to 256 colors.

❻ If you're placing line art, company logos, or icons in your HTML document, you should save these images in the GIF89a format. By doing so, you'll be able to take advantage of the interlacing and transparency features, which are explained in detail in the next chapter.

❺ If you are including photographic images in your HTML document, you should store them in JPEG format because of the smaller file size and support for full color. Some Web browsers do not directly support JPEG files, and require the reader to load them with an external JPEG viewer. Many JPEG viewers are available for free on the Internet. You can find a list of them at http://www.yahoo.com/computers_and_ Internet/Software/Graphics/.

TIP SHEET

▶ Remember that JPEG images are 24-bit color, and require the appropriate video hardware to view properly. If the user's system can only support 256 colors, the images will be automatically adjusted to 256 colors by the Web browser or external viewer through a process known as color dithering. This will always degrade the quality of the image, and may lead to results you did not anticipate. Therefore, it's best to use 24-bit JPEG images only when absolutely necessary.

▶ Images take a considerable amount of time to load in an HTML document, especially when the reader has a slow modem connection to the Internet. Try to keep your images as compact as possible. Crop the images wherever possible to show only the relevant portions, thereby reducing the image size. Color depth also plays a huge role in overall image size. Consider decreasing the number of colors to 16 or 256 if it won't adversely affect the image.

2 There are two different formats for GIF images: the GIF87 format and the GIF89a format. The first format is the original format, and is no longer widely used. The GIF89a format takes advantage of new enhancements, including transparency and interlacing, which are used extensively by HTML authors.

3 The JPEG format, developed by the Joint Photographic Experts Group, is also a cross-platform format, although it is not directly supported by all Web browsers. JPEG images can use the full spectrum of 16.7 million colors.

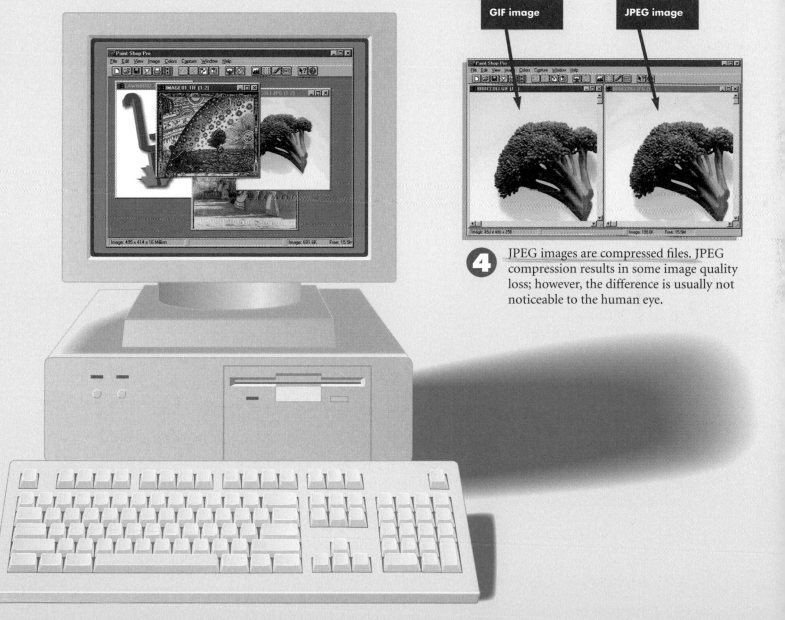

GIF image

JPEG image

4 JPEG images are compressed files. JPEG compression results in some image quality loss; however, the difference is usually not noticeable to the human eye.

How to Convert a Bitmap to a GIF File

In order to create GIF and JPEG images, you need an image editing program that can read and write in those file formats. The Paint program that comes with Windows 95 does not support GIF or JPEG. Fortunately, there are many low-cost image editing programs that do, including some free ones. In this section, you will learn how to create a GIF file by using Paint Shop Pro, an inexpensive and widely used image editing utility.

If you've got a Windows bitmap file that you'd like to use, such as your Windows wallpaper, Paint Shop Pro will help you convert it to GIF or JPEG format.

▶ **1** Start Paint Shop Pro. If you don't already have a copy of Paint Shop Pro on your system, you'll need to download a copy. An evaluation version is available on the publisher's Web site at http://www.jasc.com.

9 Choose a file name and location for your image file.

8 To save the 256-color image as a GIF file, choose Save As from the File menu or press F12. Make sure that the List Files of Type box is set to *GIF - CompuServe* and the File Sub-Format is set to *Version 89a - Interlaced*. To save this image as a JPEG file instead, set the file type to *JPG - JPEG - JFIF compliant*.

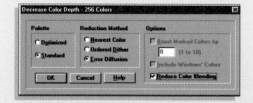

7 In the Decrease Color Depth dialog box, make sure that the standard palette is selected. In most cases, you'll want to choose Error Diffusion as your reduction method, but feel free to experiment. Press the OK button when you're ready to go.

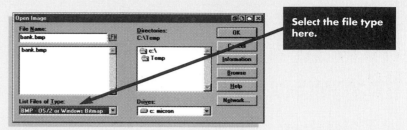

Select the file type here.

3 In the Open Image dialog box, change the value in the List Files of Type box to *BMP - OS/2 or Windows Bitmap*.

2 Open your .BMP bitmap file by choosing Open from the File menu or by pressing Ctrl+O.

4 Locate the bitmap file on your system that you want to convert, then press the OK button.

Paint tools

Bitmap image

GIF image

Status Bar

6 To decrease the number of colors used in the image, select Decrease Color Depth from the Colors menu and choose 256 colors (8-bit).

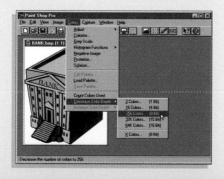

Image: 240 x 291 x 16 Million

5 Check to see how many colors your .BMP image uses. The number of colors used is displayed in the lower-left corner of the status bar. If it's 256 colors or less, you can save this image as a GIF file. If it's more than 256 colors, you'll either need to decrease the number of colors or save the image as a JPEG file.

How to Add an Image to Your HTML Document

O nce you've got the image file prepared, the next step is to place it in your HTML document with markup tags. Images in HTML are included by using the <IMG> tag. This page will cover the basic elements and attributes used when including an <IMG> tag in your document.

▶ **1** Locate the place in your document where you'd like to insert the image.

▶ **If you want to link to images that are not your own, be sure to get permission from the copyright holder first.**

▶ **You should always use ALT to specify alternate text for an image, so that users without graphical capability will understand what the image is showing.**

`<IMG>`

2 You can place images in your HTML document by using the <IMG> tag. To insert an image into your HTML document, type <**IMG**>. There is no closing </IMG> tag.

`<IMG SRC="logo.gif">`

3 Now you need to specify the URL of the image to load by placing the SRC (source) attribute within the <IMG> tag. If you store your images in the same directory as your HTML files, the URL can simply be the file name of the image. For example, to insert a GIF file named *logo.gif* into your HTML document, you would type <**IMG SRC="logo.gif"**>.

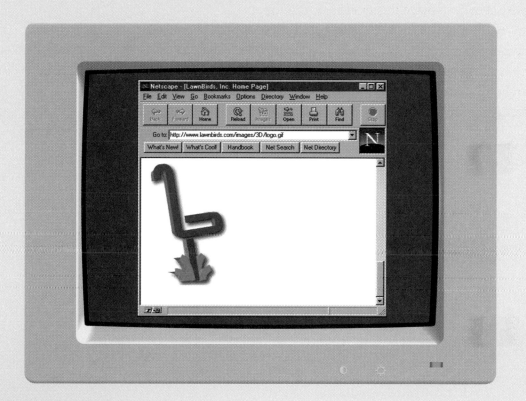

Alternate text

Welcome to LawnBirds, Inc.

LawnBirds logo

We're the worldwide leading manufacturer and distributor of avian lawn ornaments. For over forty years, our company has built and sold our product with the kind of pride, love and warmth that only a **quality** lawn ornament can inspire. When you place a LawnBird brand lawn ornament in front of your house, you're saying a lot about the type of person you are.

5 The ALT attribute allows you to create alternate text for your image that will be shown to users who have browsers that do not support graphics. Some browsers will also display the alternate text while the image is loading. To specify the alternate text, type **ALT**=, followed by the text in quotes. For example, adding alternate text would change the above image tag to <IMG SRC="images/logo.gif" ALT="The LawnBirds, Inc. logo in stunning 3-D.">.

`<IMG SRC="images/logo.gif">`

4 To link to images that are not in the same directory as the HTML document, use relative URLs to locate them. For example, if you stored the above logo.gif file in a subdirectory called *images* in your HTML documents folder, you would type <**IMG SRC="images/logo.gif"**>.

How to Format Images in HTML

As you've learned, it's very easy to include an image in your HTML document. However, simply including an image is only the first step. HTML provides you with several ways to format your image inside your document. You can align your image with the margins to allow text to flow around it. You can also specify the size you'd like the image to be, allowing the reader's Web browser to scale the image accordingly.

TIP SHEET

▶ **You can determine the height and width of an image by opening the file in Paint Shop Pro. The number of pixels in the height and width of the image are displayed in the status bar.**

▶ **It's always a good idea to specify the height and width of your image, even if you don't want to scale it to a different size. When you indicate a size in the <IMG> tag, many browsers will insert a rectangle as a placeholder while the image downloads. This will allow users to read the text of your document immediately, instead of having to wait for the images to download first.**

▶ **1** To specify the alignment of an image, use the ALIGN attribute inside the <IMG> tag.

6 There are a number of enhancements to the <IMG> tag. Netscape provides many extensions for greater layout control. Also, a new HTML3 feature that is not yet widely implemented is the <FIG> (figure) tag, which is much more versatile than the <IMG> tag. Both the Netscape and <FIG> tags will be covered in later chapters.

`<IMG SRC="logo.gif" ALIGN=BOTTOM>`

2 To align the image above the text that surrounds it, type **ALIGN=BOTTOM**. This sets the bottom of the image equal to the baseline of the text. Likewise, to align the image below the surrounding text, type **ALIGN=TOP**. You can also align the middle of the image to the text baseline by typing **ALIGN=MIDDLE**.

`<IMG SRC="logo.gif" ALIGN=LEFT>`

3 To force text to wrap around an image, type **ALIGN=LEFT** inside the <IMG> tag. This will align the image with the left margin of the document, and text will flow around it, beginning with the current paragraph.

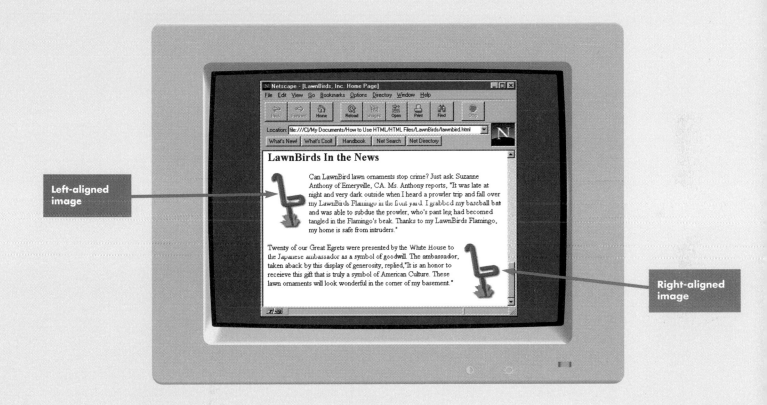

Left-aligned image

Right-aligned image

`<IMG SRC="logo.gif" ALIGN=RIGHT>`

4 To place the image in the right margin of your document, type **ALIGN=RIGHT**.

`<IMG SRC="logo.gif" HEIGHT=150 WIDTH=100>`

5 You can specify the height and width of your image. If you specify a different height and width than the actual image, the browser will scale the image to fit your settings. To set the height, place your cursor in the <IMG> tag and type **HEIGHT=**, followed by the height of the image in pixels. To specify the width of the image, type **WIDTH=**.

TRY IT!

Once again, here is an opportunity to put the skills you've learned in the past few chapters to the test. Your client, LawnBirds, Inc., is asking you to redesign their home page on the World Wide Web. This time, they want to include their corporate logo on the page, along with background information on the company. In addition, they want to showcase brief descriptions of their top-selling products.

Using the tricks you learned for using images and lists, you'll create the document from scratch using Notepad, and finish with a complete, professional HTML document for LawnBirds, Inc.

Start
Notepad.

2

Turn Word Wrap on.

3

Type in the first few lines of your HTML document as shown here, pressing Enter after each one.

4

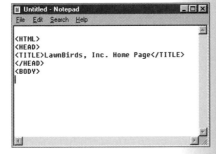

Type in a headline, and then press Enter.

5

Now we'll insert the LawnBirds logo. First, you would preview the image using a graphics editor capable of displaying GIF and JPEG images. Since you probably don't have a copy of the LawnBirds logo on your system, you can use any image you like in its place. Save the file as logo.gif or logo.jpg, depending on the file type.

6

Image: 203 x 153 x 256

Note the image's height and width in pixels and then write these numbers down. They'll be used later.

7

`<IMG>`

Now we'll insert the LawnBirds logo. Type <IMG> to insert an image tag.

8

`<IMG SRC="logo.gif">`

Inside the <IMG> tag, type SRC= followed by the file name, **logo.gif**, in quotes.

9

`ALT="LawnBirds logo">`

To create some alternate text for browsers that don't display graphics, type **ALT="LawnBirds logo"** inside the <IMG> tag.

10

`.gif" ALT="LawnBirds logo" ALIGN=LEFT>`

To align the image with the left margin, type **ALIGN=LEFT** inside the <IMG> tag.

Continue to next page ▶

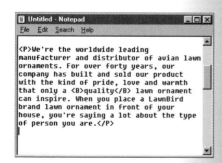

TRY IT!

Continue
below

14

LawnBirds, Inc. wants to use this home page to
give customers quick descriptions of their available products. You've decided that this is the
perfect opportunity to make creative use of a
definition list. The product names will be formatted as definition terms, and the product descriptions will be formatted as the definitions
themselves.

11

`HEIGHT=153 WIDTH=203`

Type the height and width of the image
inside the <IMG> tag.

15

`<P>`

First, type <P> to start a new paragraph.

12

`<P>`

On the next line, type <P> to start a
paragraph.

16

Type in a
brief intro-
duction ex-
plaining what
the list will
contain.
Then type
</P> and press Enter.

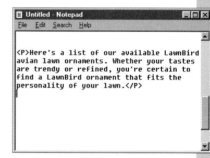

```
Untitled - Notepad
File  Edit  Search  Help

<P>Here's a list of our available LawnBird
avian lawn ornaments. Whether your tastes
are trendy or refined, you're certain to
find a LawnBird ornament that fits the
personality of your lawn.</P>
```

13

Type the en-
tire first
paragraph.
Remember,
you do not
need to press
Enter to start
new lines of text. At the end of the
paragraph, type </P> and press Enter.

```
Untitled - Notepad
File  Edit  Search  Help

<P>We're the worldwide leading
manufacturer and distributor of avian lawn
ornaments. For over forty years, our
company has built and sold our product
with the kind of pride, love and warmth
that only a <B>quality</B> lawn ornament
can inspire. When you place a LawnBird
brand lawn ornament in front of your
house, you're saying a lot about the type
of person you are.</P>
```

17

`<DL>`

To begin the Definition List, type
<DL> and then press Enter.

18

```
<DT>The Flamingo
|
```

Type <DT>,
followed by the name of the first
LawnBirds product. This line is a
definition term. Press Enter to start
a new line.

19

```
<DD>The flamingo is our premier lawn bird.
Tall, elegant, graceful, yet whimsical
too. With its colorful plumage, the
flamingo has added charm to lawns and
gardens for many years.
|
```

Type <DD>,
followed by
the first product description. This line
is the definition. When you're finished
typing it in, press Enter.

20

Repeat the
previous two
steps for each
of the prod-
ucts and
product
descriptions
in the
LawnBirds Line.

21

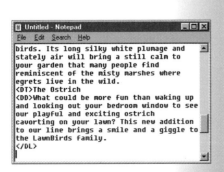

Type </DL>
to close the
definition
list, and then
press Enter.

22

LawnBirds, Inc. also wants to include a list
of ways to contact the company and order
its products. The best way to present this
information is by using an unordered list.

23

```
<UL>
|
```

Type <UL>
to begin the list, and then press Enter.

24

```
<LH><STRONG>How to Contact LawnBirds,
Inc.</STRONG></LH>
|
```

To create a list heading and make it
stand out from the list items, type
<LH><STRONG>How to Contact
LawnBirds, Inc.</STRONG></LH>.
The *<STRONG>* tag is a logical
markup tag that tells the Web browser
to display this text with strong emphasis. Now press Enter.

25

```
<LI>Phone: 1-800-555-LAWN
```

Type <LI> followed by the first line of
contact information, then press Enter.

Continue to next page ▶

TRY IT!

Continue
below

29

```
</HTML>
```

Type </HTML> to mark the end of the
document.

26

```
<LI>Phone: 1-800-555-LAWN
<LI>FAX: 1-999-555-2323
<LI>EMail: sales@lawnbirds.com
```

Repeat the
previous step for each of the elements
in the list.

30

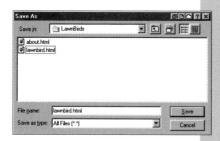

Save the file
in Notepad.
Choose a
meaningful
file name,
such as
lawnbird.html.

27

```
</UL>
```

After you've
entered the last list item, type </UL>
and press Enter.

31

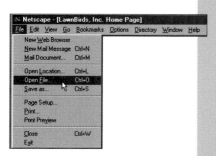

Load the new
HTML docu-
ment using
the Open File
option in
your Web
browser.

28

```
</BODY>
```

Type </BODY> to mark the end of the
body section of the document, then
press Enter.

CHAPTER 9

Advanced Graphics Techniques

 Now that you've got a handle on the basic concepts behind using graphics with HTML, you're ready to tackle some of the more advanced techniques. In this chapter, you'll learn some very cool tricks for making the most out of images on the Web.

Among the secrets covered are using background images, taking advantage of transparency with GIF files, and how to used interlaced images to make your Web pages appear to load faster.

In this chapter, you'll also learn about the new figure element, which adds a whole range of new options for using and formatting images in HTML.

How to Change Colors in HTML

U p until now, your HTML documents have been limited to pretty basic colors—black text and a white or gray background, depending on the Web browser being used. As an HTML author you have the ability to change the colors of the text and background of your document when you feel it's necessary.

RGB values in decimal notation

1 Colors in HTML are designated by their RGB values. RGB is a measurement of the levels of red, green, and blue in a particular color. The value of each can range from 0 to 255, yielding a total of 16.7 million different combinations. For example, true red has a value of 255 in its red channel and values of 0 in both its blue and green channels. Black has values of 0 for all three channels, and white has values of 255 for all of its RGB channels.

`ALINK=#ff0000`

8 Finally, you can set the color for active links. A link is only briefly displayed in its active state when the user clicks on the hyperlink text. The active color is essentially a way of giving momentary feedback to the user to let them know that they have selected a link. To change the active link text color, type **ALINK=#** followed by the appropriate RGB values.

`VLINK=#ebebeb`

7 To set the color for hyperlinks that you have already visited, type **VLINK=#**, followed by the RGB values for the color you have chosen.

TIP SHEET

▶ **Try to keep your background colors simple. The best colors for backgrounds are pastel or soft colors. Bright colors are a bad choice as a background, because the text will almost always be difficult to read.**

▶ **With 16.7 million colors available for both the background and text, there are over *280 trillion* possible combinations. Unfortunately, only a handful of those actually produce readable text. Don't go overboard when changing your color settings—make sure your document is easy to read and understand.**

2 To make things even more confusing, HTML requires you to specify the RGB values in hexadecimal notation, which will be familiar to programmers but difficult for everyone else. Fortunately, there are a number of free color calculation programs available on the Internet that will compute the necessary values for you. One of the best is HTML Color Reference, which is available at ftp://ftp.winternet.com/users/faz/HCR/hcrv2all.zip.

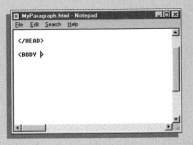

3 Remember the <BODY> tag from the beginning of your HTML document? Background image information is stored inside the <BODY> tag. In Notepad, place the cursor inside the tag, after the word *BODY*.

`<BODY BGCOLOR=#0000ff>`

4 To specify a background color for your HTML document, type BGCOLOR=# followed by the RGB value of the color in hexadecimal notation. For example, to set the background color to blue, you would type BGCOLOR=#0000ff. That sets the red and green channels to 0 and the blue channel to 255 (*ff* is hexadecimal for *255*).

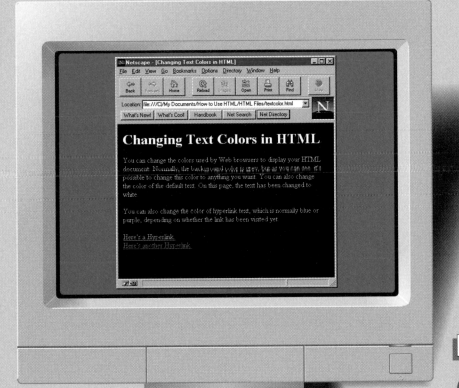

`<BODY BGCOLOR=#0000ff TEXT=#ffffff>`

5 Setting your background to a dark color can cause problems with readability, because by default text is displayed in black. Fortunately, you can also change the text color. To specify a particular color for normal text in your HTML document, place the cursor inside the <BODY> tag and type TEXT=#, followed by an RGB value. For example, to specify a text color of white (to complement a dark background color, such as blue), you would type TEXT=#ffffff.

`LINK=#ffff3f`

6 Web browsers also use colors for hyperlink text. Hypertext link text can actually be one of two colors. Typically, unvisited hyperlinks are blue and hyperlinks that you've already visited are purple. Again, using an RGB value, you can set these colors to your own specification. To change the normal hyperlink color, insert the cursor inside the <BODY> tag and type LINK=#, followed by the RGB values for the color.

How to Create an Interlaced GIF File

If your HTML document contains a lot of images, it will take a while to load in some Web browsers, especially if the reader has a slow Internet connection. If your images are especially large, it will take a long time for them to display.

One way to get around this problem is to use interlaced GIF images. Interlaced images are loaded by Web browsers so that they appear to slowly come into focus. The result is that the reader initially sees a low resolution version of the final image, and will at least have a general idea of what it looks like before it is finished loading. Used properly, this technique will make your HTML documents appear to load faster.

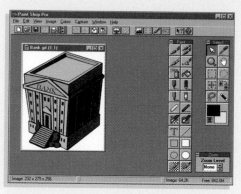

▶ ❶ Creating an interlaced image is actually quite simple. The first step is to open your image using an editor that supports GIF files, such as Paint Shop Pro.

2 To make sure the image is saved as an interlaced image, first choose Save As from the File menu.

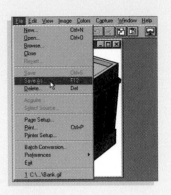

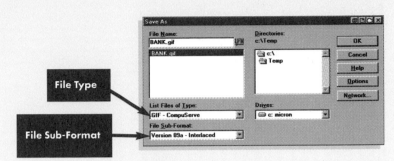

File Type

File Sub-Format

3 Set the File Type to **GIF - CompuServe** and the File Sub-Format to **Version 89a - Interlaced**.

An interlaced GIF "paints" itself as it is loaded.

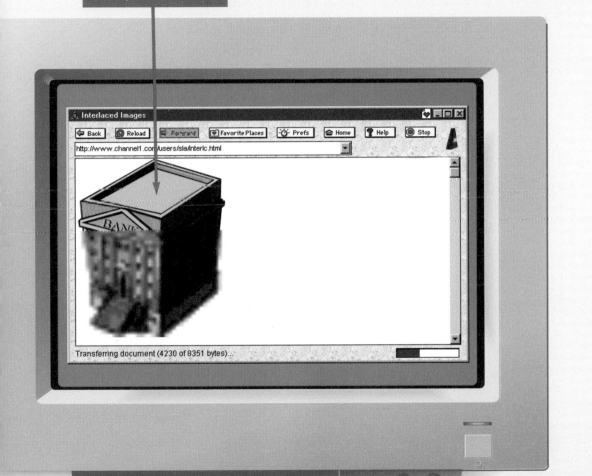

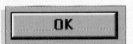

OK

4 Click on the OK button to save the image as an interlaced GIF file.

5 If you're using an image editor other than Paint Shop Pro, check the documentation for exact instructions on how to set the image options to be interlaced.

How to Create a Background Image in HTML

In your travels on the World Wide Web, you've probably run across pages that use a background image, which looks similar to a watermark. Instead of a solid background, an image is tiled repeatedly in the background of the Web browser, like the Wallpaper on your Windows desktop.

HTML allows you to specify an image as background wallpaper for your Web page. In this section, you will learn how.

▶ ❶ The first thing to do is to select an image to use as your background wallpaper. It's a good idea to choose a very low-contrast image with few colors, since the text of your page will appear on top of the image. Corporate logos or simple repeating patterns make excellent choices for background wallpaper.

Change the contrast of the image here.

Paint Shop Pro provides a live preview of your changes.

❼ In the Brightness/Contrast dialog, you can lower the contrast level by clicking on the down arrow next to the box marked Contrast or by typing in a negative percentage value. Click on the OK button when you're finished.

TIP SHEET

▶ **The best images to use in the background are simple, small images with muted colors, such as gray. Bright or high-contrast images will make your HTML document hard to read.**

▶ **There are several free background tile images available at various sites for your personal use. The Yahoo Internet Directory has a list of sites that provide images. Go to http://www.yahoo.com/ Computers_and_Internet/ Internet/World_Wide_Web/ Programming/Background/ for the list. Always make sure you have rights to use the image before you include it in your HTML document.**

2 Remember the <BODY> tag from the beginning of your HTML document? Background image information is stored inside the <BODY> tag. In Notepad, place the cursor inside the tag, after the word *BODY*.

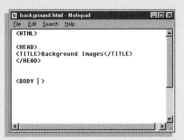

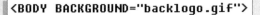

3 Type **BACKGROUND="** followed by the file name of your image and a closing quotation mark. For example, to specify a file named backlogo.gif as your background image, you would type **BACKGROUND="backlogo.gif"**.

Text appears on top of the background image.

4 Preview your HTML document with the background image to make sure that the text is still readable.

5 If it's too hard to read, you'll need to lower the contrast of your graphic using image editing software, or choose another graphic.

6 To lower the contrast of your image, open it in Paint Shop Pro and click on the Colors menu. Then choose Adjust, followed by Brightness/Contrast from the drop-down menu.

How to Create a Transparent Image in HTML

One of the coolest graphical effects in use on the Web today is transparency. One of the enhancements to the GIF file format was the addition of support for a transparent color. Simply put, you can specify one color in your GIF image to be invisible.

As long as the Web browser supports this capability, the parts of a GIF image that contain the transparent color won't be rendered—the background portion of your Web page will show through instead. This functionality is ideal for pages that use background wallpaper, as well as for nonrectangular images such as corporate logos.

1 Open your GIF file in an image editing program that supports transparency, such as Paint Shop Pro.

7 If you're using an image editing program other than Paint Shop Pro, don't worry—the same steps for setting the transparent color usually apply. Refer to your program documentation for the exact details.

6 Click on the Options button in the Save As dialog box. In the GIF Transparency Options dialog, choose Set the Transparency Value to the Background Color. If for some reason you did not use the background color as your transparent color, you'll need to set the Transparency value to *s* specific color index (see the Paint Shop Pro documentation for details). Then save the document.

2 Choose a color to be the transparent color. All of the pixels in your image with this color will not be displayed when viewed in a Web browser. In Paint Shop Pro, it's easiest to set this color to be the background color as well.

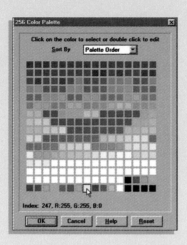

3 Using the paint tools, fill the portions of the image that you want to be invisible with the transparent color. Be sure to fill all the areas that need to be transparent with this color, including spaces between letters.

Images using transparency allow the background to show through.

Images without transparency obscure the background completely.

4 Make sure that the transparent color is not used elsewhere in the image. Any pixel with this color will become invisible when viewed with a Web browser.

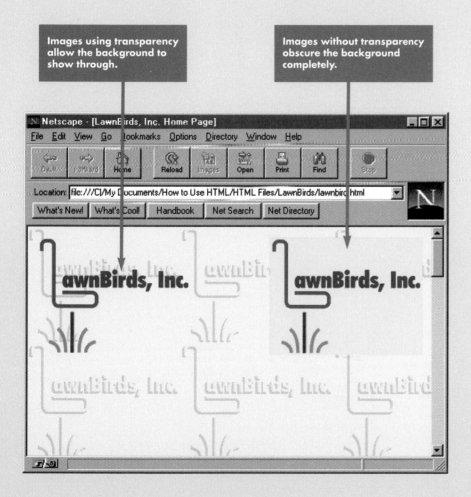

5 Choose Save As from the File menu.

How to Use Figures

Figures are new to HTML3. They work very similar to images, but give HTML authors much more flexibility than the <IMG> tag. The figure element gives you greater control over the formatting of the image, as well as the alternate text that appears in browsers that can't view images.

Figures have been introduced to HTML3 as a partial replacement for the <IMG> tag. Large images should use the <FIG> tag because of the added flexibility. Small graphics, such as bullets and icons, should continue to be placed with <IMG>.

You should be careful when deciding to use figures in your HTML documents. This new feature is not yet supported by any of the major Web browsers, and it is unclear if this new element will be widely accepted and used.

 1 To insert a figure in your HTML document, place the cursor anywhere inside the body section and type <**FIG SRC=**>.

 `<OVERLAY SRC="utah.gif">`

7 To add an overlay to a figure, type <OVER-LAY SRC=, followed by the file name of the overlay image in quotes. Then close the tag. To add an overlay that highlighted the state of Utah in the previous example, you would type <OVERLAY SRC="utah.gif">. The image itself would be mostly transparent, with the exception of Utah, to allow the underlying figure graphic to show through.

TIP SHEET

▸ Although the <FIG> element is part of the working HTML3 specification, it is not widely supported by Web browsers. Before including figures in your documents, make sure that your readers will be able to view them.

```
<FIG SRC="salesmap.gif">
```

2 Add the name of the image file to be displayed after the equal sign and enclose it with quotes. For example, to include an image named *salesmap.gif* in your HTML document, you would type **<FIG SRC="salesmap.gif">**.

```
map.gif" ALIGN=LEFT>
```

3 As with the <IMG> tag, you can align images displayed with <FIG>. To do this, add the ALIGN= attribute followed by a standard alignment value. For example, you can align the figure along the left side of your HTML document by typing **ALIGN=LEFT** inside the <FIG> tag.

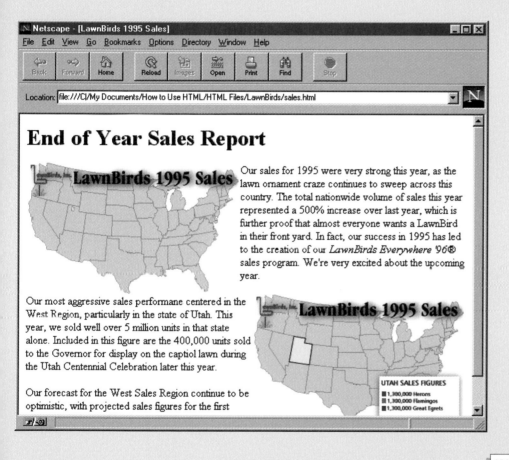

```
<FIG SRC="salesmap.gif" ALIGN=LEFT>

This text will appear instead of the Figure
in <EM>text-only</EM> browsers.

</FIG>
```

4 The alternate text for non-graphical browsers is placed between the <FIG> and </FIG> tags. This text may be formatted using all of the normal character formatting attributes, such as bold, italic, emphasis, and strong.

```
<CAPTION>1995 Sales by State</CAPTION>
```

6 Figures can also use a powerful new feature called *overlays*. Overlays work in the same way as transparency overlays do—each overlay contains minor changes to the original, and is placed on top of it. Multiple overlays can be stacked to show a progression of change.

5 Figures allow the addition of captions and credits. To add a caption to an image, place your caption text between a <CAPTION> and </CAPTION> tag pair anywhere after the <FIG> tag, but before the closing </FIG> tag. For example, to add a caption to the Sales Map figure, you would type **<CAPTION>1995 LawnBirds Sales by State</CAPTION>**.

CHAPTER 10

Getting Feedback with Forms

Up until now, HTML has been a one-way street. That is, we've only covered the tools to create and publish information for end users to read. But what about feedback and interaction? The World Wide Web isn't just about publishing. It's designed for communication, which is a street that travels in more than one direction.

The biggest tool for allowing your readers to communicate with you via the Web is the *HTML form*. Forms are special collections of markup tags that work with Web servers to produce a means of obtaining whatever information you need from visitors to your Web site. In this chapter, we'll discover how to create a basic form in HTML, as well as how to use all the available types of input fields at your disposal. Finally, we'll discuss some basic principles behind CGI, the Common Gateway Interface, which is the system behind the scenes that makes forms work.

How to Create a Simple Form

If the whole concept of filling out forms makes you bleary-eyed or fills your head with horrible visions of standing in line at the Department of Motor Vehicles, don't worry. Fill-out forms in HTML are easy, quick, and painless. In fact, you can create a simple fill-out form in just a few simple steps.

1 Type <**FORM**> in your HTML document.

6 To specify a single-line text field, enter **TYPE=TEXT** inside the <INPUT> tag.

```
<FORM METHOD=POST>
```

2 Each <FORM> tag has two important attributes that need to be set: Method and Action. The *Method* attribute indicates how the information inside the form will be transferred to the Web server. There are two choices for Method: GET and POST. The critical difference between the two is that the POST method tells the server to process the form line by line, while the GET method tells the server to process the entire form as one long concatenated string of values. You'll almost always want to use the POST method with your forms.

```
METHOD=POST ACTION="../cgi-bin/process-data">
```

3 The *Action* attribute tells the server what to do with the data contained in the form. This attribute usually contains the URL of a special program designed to process the data. You'll learn a little more about how this works at the end of the chapter.

```
<FORM METHOD=POST ACTION="../cgi-bin/process-
<P>Last Name:
```

4 Enter your form labels using normal HTML markup codes. For example, to create a label to prompt the user to enter their last name at the top of the form, type <P>**Last Name:**.

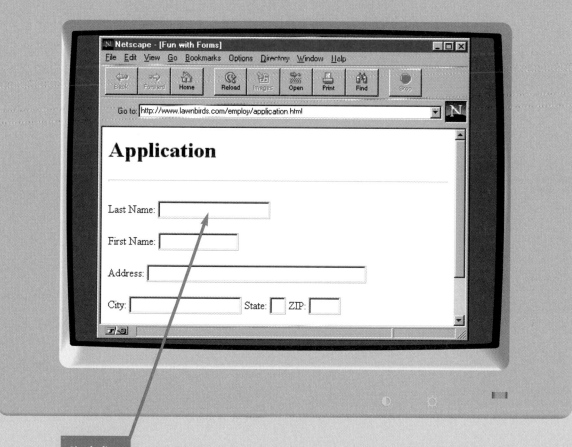

Single-line text field

```
<P>Last Name:
<INPUT>
```

5 To insert a data field to allow the user to enter information into the form, type <INPUT>. This tells the Web browser to place a data field in the document and to accept user input. There are several types of input fields available. One of the simplest types is the *single-line text field*.

Continue to next page ▶

How to Create a Simple Form (Continued)

```
<INPUT TYPE=text NAME="lastname">
```

▶ **7** Each input field needs to be assigned a name, so that it can be distinguished from other input fields. You can name the input field anything you like, but the name should be kept short and should not contain any spaces or special characters. For example, to name the above field *lastname*, type NAME="lastname" inside the <INPUT> tag.

TIP SHEET

▶ **Long forms usually work best when placed in their own HTML documents. If your form requires a lot of input, create a new HTML document just for the form and then create a hyperlink to it from your main page. This will eliminate clutter and confusion.**

▶ **You're not limited to just input fields in your form. You can use all the normal HTML paragraph and character formatting codes. It's often a good idea to place brief paragraphs in front of groups of input fields to help explain what needs to be entered in the form.**

```
</FORM>
```

 11 Type </FORM> on a new line to close the form.

```
NAME="lastname" SIZE="20">
```

8 You can specify the maximum length of a text field with the size attribute by typing **SIZE=**, followed by the length in quotes. For example, to limit the length of the lastname field to 20 characters, type **SIZE="20"** inside the <INPUT> tag.

Submit Query

9 The last two input items that every form should have are the Submit and Reset buttons. The *Submit button* is pressed by the user when the form is completed, and sends all of the information to the server. To include a Submit button in your form, type **<INPUT TYPE=SUBMIT>** near the bottom of the form. The Submit button is a required element—without it, the form cannot be processed.

Reset

10 The *Reset button* allows the user to clear all of the fields in the form at once and reset them to their initial values so that new information can be added. Although the Reset button is not required, it is strongly recommended. To include it in your form, type **<INPUT TYPE=RESET>**.

How to Use Input Fields in Forms

In many cases, simple text fields aren't enough when it comes to specifying the type of information you want to receive from your forms. Fortunately, HTML forms are very flexible, and include many different types of data fields.

```
<INPUT NAME="password" TYPE=password>
```

▶ **1** You can insert a *password field* into your form. This acts like a single-line text field, but hides the input by displaying asterisks (**) in place of the actual characters entered. To insert a password field into your form, type <INPUT NAME="**password**" TYPE=**PASSWORD**>. You can specify the maximum length of the password using the SIZE attribute.

```
<INPUT NAME="attachment" TYPE=file>
```

6 You can add file attachments to the form by using the *file type*. This allows users to attach a file to the form by either typing the file name or selecting it from a browse dialog. To insert a file attachment field, type <INPUT NAME="**attachment**" TYPE=**file**>.

```
<P>Please choose one:<BR>
 <INPUT NAME="sex" TYPE=radio>Male
 <INPUT NAME="sex" TYPE=radio>Female
 <INPUT NAME="sex" TYPE=radio>Not Sure
</P>
```

5 To insert a radio group into your form, type <INPUT NAME= "**groupname**" TYPE=**radio** VALUE="**value1**">. Each item in the group is entered with separate <INPUT> tags and unique VALUE attributes, but all of the items in the same radio button group should have the same NAME attribute.

```
<INPUT NAME="score" TYPE=RANGE MIN=0 MAX=100>
```

2 *Range fields* allow the user to select a numeric value that falls between two predetermined maximum and minimum values. These values are set using the MIN and MAX attributes. For example, to insert a range field that allows the user to assign a test score value between 0 and 100, type **<INPUT NAME="score" TYPE=RANGE MIN=0 MAX=100>**.

☑ Check here to receive our newsletter.

3 *Checkbox fields* allow the user to select or deselect an item. You can also initialize the field to be selected by setting the VALUE attribute to "checked". The label for the checkbox is typed in immediately after the <INPUT> tag. For example, you might include a checkbox field on your form to allow users to specify whether or not they'd like to receive a newsletter. To insert this field into your form, type **<INPUT NAME="getnews" TYPE=checkbox VALUE= "checked">Check here to receive our newsletter.**

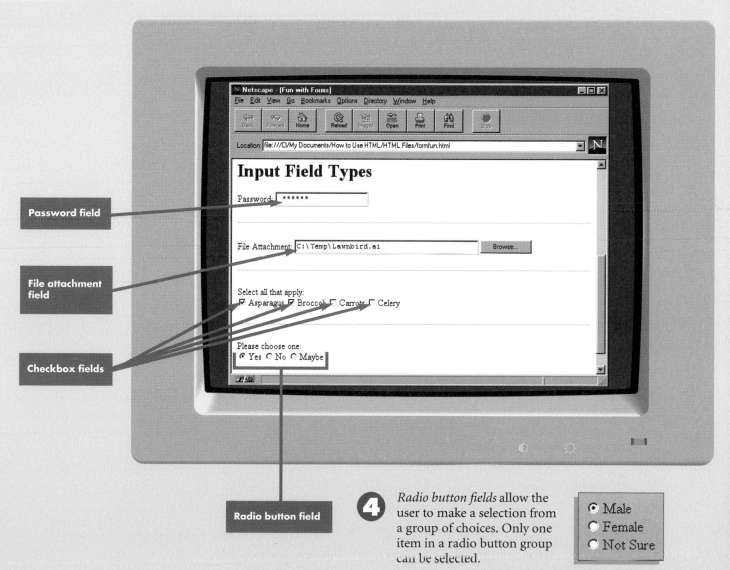

Password field

File attachment field

Checkbox fields

Radio button field

4 *Radio button fields* allow the user to make a selection from a group of choices. Only one item in a radio button group can be selected.

⦿ Male
○ Female
○ Not Sure

Continue to next page ▶

How to Use Input Fields in Forms (Continued)

▶ **7** You can also insert a *free-form field* for text, which allows the user to enter more than just a single line of text. Instead of using the <INPUT> tag, use the <TEXTAREA> and </TEXTAREA> tag pair.

`</SELECT>`

12 When you've finished typing in all of the option items, type </SELECT>.

```
<TEXTAREA NAME="comments" ROWS=6 COLS=65>
</TEXTAREA>
```

8 The <TEXTAREA> tag accepts several rows of input, up to the maximum you specify using the ROWS attribute. You can also specify the number of columns (the line width) in the TEXTAREA field with the COLS attribute. For example, to create a field to allow a user to enter comments, you would type **<TEXTAREA NAME= "comments" ROWS=6 COLS=65>**. This would leave room for six lines of up to 65 characters each.

9 Sometimes you'll want to include a selection menu on your form. This allows you to present the user with a large number of choices without using up too much space on your form. The menu can allow either a single or multiple-choice selection.

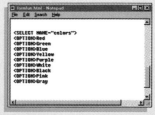

```
<SELECT NAME="colors">
```

10 To insert a selection menu, use the <SELECT> and </SELECT> tag pair. As with the <INPUT> tag, you need to assign a NAME attribute for your selection menu. For example, to create a selection menu that allows the user to choose a color, type **<SELECT NAME="color">**. If you want to allow multiple selections to be made, insert the attribute MULTIPLE inside the <SELECT> tag.

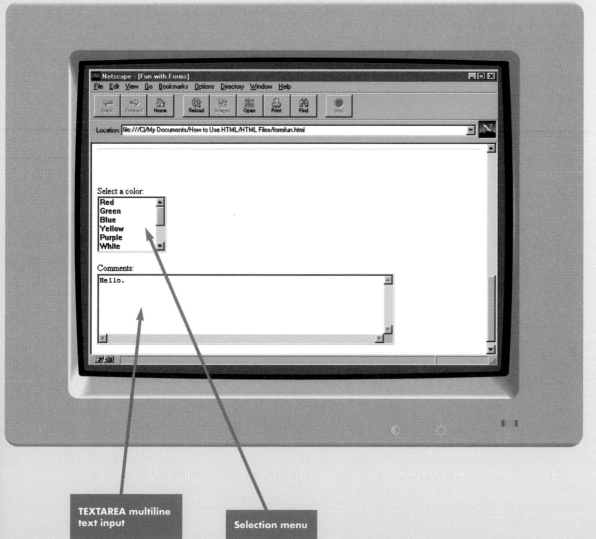

TEXTAREA multiline text input

Selection menu

11 Each item in a selection menu is typed in using the <OPTION> tag (much like the unordered list from Chapter 7). Enter each menu choice on a separate line.

How CGI Makes Your Forms Work

Of course, everything you learned about forms wouldn't amount to much if there weren't a way to process the information they contained. There is a way, and it's called *CGI*, which is short for *common gateway interface*.

CGI is a universal way to execute programs on the Web. These programs are known as *CGI scripts*, and are designed to process data submitted via forms from Web browsers of all types. CGI scripts can be written and compiled using a variety of different programming languages, such as Perl or Visual Basic. The language used depends on the type of server that the CGI script needs to be run on.

In this section, we'll take a brief overview of how CGI works behind the scenes to handle data from your forms.

1 The user supplies data by filling out the form, and then presses the Submit button.

6 The server sends the new information along to the Web browser, which displays it.

```
<FORM METHOD=POST ACTION="../cgi-bin/process-data"
```

2 The browser sends the data fields from the form to a CGI script. The appropriate script is specified with the ACTION attribute in the <FORM> tag.

3 The CGI script processes the data supplied by the browser.

4 At this point, the CGI script may update a database on the server, instruct the server to perform additional functions, or even execute additional CGI scripts.

5 The CGI script finishes and returns information to the server, usually in the form of a new HTML document that is created by the script.

CHAPTER 11

Using Tables

The most significant addition to HTML3 is support for tables. Tables give HTML authors much greater control over the display and layout of their pages. Typically, you would use tables to display any type of data that looks best in rows and columns. A good rule of thumb is if it looks good as a spreadsheet, then it belongs in a table.

Tables aren't just for numerical data. They can be used to creatively solve a number of challenges with presenting information in HTML. Tables can be used to enhance a number of existing HTML elements, such as lists and forms. You can even use tables to gain precision control over the layout of your HTML document.

Of course, there's always a catch. Tables are notoriously difficult and tedious to create in HTML. And because the specification for HTML3 is still not final, some of the formatting details for tables are subject to change.

How to Create a Simple Table

Creating a simple table in HTML is fairly straightforward. All you need to do is supply the data. The client-side Web browser takes care of all the dirty work by determining how to display it.

The key thing to remember about tables in HTML is that they are organized in rows, which go horizontally from left to right. Once you begin to think of the data you want to place in your table in terms of rows, you'll be all set to perform some HTML wizardry.

In this section, you'll get started by stepping through the process of creating your first table in HTML.

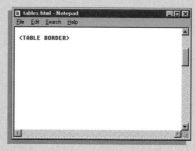

1 Type <**TABLE BORDER**> in your HTML document to create a table with a thin border around all of the table cells.

`</TABLE>`

8 Type in your remaining data, using the <TD> and </TD> tags to separate each cell and the <TR> and </TR> tags to separate each row. When you're finished, type </**TABLE**> to signal the end of the table.

`<TD>$20,300</TD>`

7 Now you can start adding the actual table data cell by cell using the <TD> and </TD> tag pair. To enter the data in the first cell of the second row, type <TD> followed by the actual data and the closing </TD> tag.

```
<CAPTION>Fourth Quarter Sales</CAPTION>
```

2 You can type in a caption for your table, which most browsers will display at the top. It's sometimes easier to think of the caption as the title of your table. Type <**CAPTION**>, followed by the actual text of your table caption. Then type </**CAPTION**> to close the tag.

```
<TABLE BORDER>
<CAPTION>Fourth Quarter Sales</CAPTION>
<TR>
```

3 Tables are built row by row using the <TR> and </TR> tag pair. To start your first table row, type <**TR**>.

Caption

Table heading

```
<TH>Last Name</TH>
```

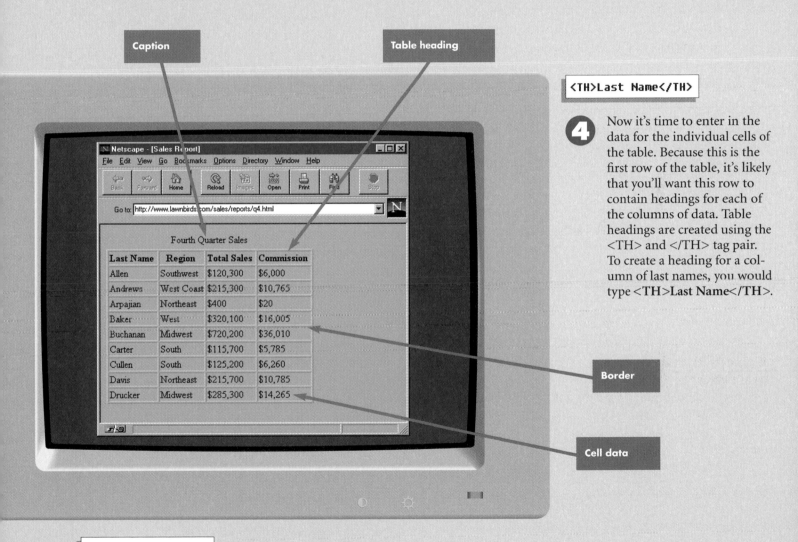

Netscape - [Sales Report]

File Edit View Go Bookmarks Options Directory Window Help

Back | Forward | Home | Reload | Images | Open | Print | Find | Stop

Go to: http://www.lawnbirds.com/sales/reports/q4.html

Fourth Quarter Sales

Last Name	Region	Total Sales	Commission
Allen	Southwest	$120,300	$6,000
Andrews	West Coast	$215,300	$10,765
Arpajian	Northeast	$400	$20
Baker	West	$320,100	$16,005
Buchanan	Midwest	$720,200	$36,010
Carter	South	$115,700	$5,785
Cullen	South	$125,200	$6,260
Davis	Northeast	$215,700	$10,785
Drucker	Midwest	$285,300	$14,265

Border

Cell data

4 Now it's time to enter in the data for the individual cells of the table. Because this is the first row of the table, it's likely that you'll want this row to contain headings for each of the columns of data. Table headings are created using the <TH> and </TH> tag pair. To create a heading for a column of last names, you would type <**TH**>**Last Name**</**TH**>.

```
<TR>

<TH>Last Name</TH>

</TR>
```

6 After you've completed your first row, type </TR> to finish it. Since you'll be adding another row immediately after it, you can type <TR> on the next line to start the new row.

5 You can type all of your column headings one after another, each contained in its own <TH> and </TH> tag pair.

How to Format Tables

Because HTML is a markup language and not a layout language, the actual display of HTML tables is left up to the Web browser. The height and width of the individual cells are calculated by the browser based on their contents. In general, browsers do a good job of displaying table contents all by themselves. Sometimes, however, you'll want to exercise a little more control over how your tables are displayed. HTML3's table formatting codes let you do just that.

1 To create a table with no border at all, simply type <**TABLE**>. You can also give your table a 3-D beveled look by adjusting the size of the outside border. This feature is only supported by Netscape browsers. To adjust the size of the outside table border, use the BORDER attribute. For example, to create a table with a border that is 8 pixels wide, type <**TABLE BORDER=8**>.

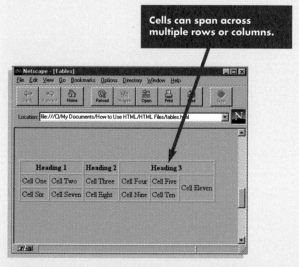

6 Sometimes you'll want an individual cell to span across multiple columns or rows. This is easy to do using the ROWSPAN and COLSPAN attributes inside the cell's <TD> tag. To force a cell to span vertically down across three rows, type <**TD ROWSPAN=3**>. To force a cell to span horizontally from left to right across several columns, use the COLSPAN attribute inside the <TD> tag. For example, to span a cell across two columns, type <**TD COLSPAN=2**>.

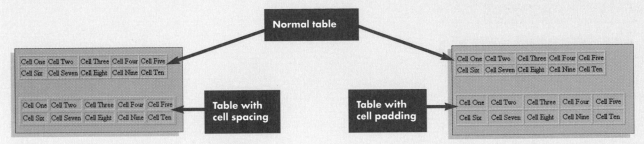

2 Netscape also adds extensions to give you even greater control over the borders and spacing of the cells inside your table. To change the size of the internal borders, add the CELLSPACING attribute to your <TABLE> tag. For example, to create a table with a wide internal border, type <TABLE BORDER CELLSPACING=5>.

3 You can also "pad" the individual cells of your table to add space on all sides. This keeps the border from running up against the actual cell contents. It's very useful if you plan on including images inside your table. To add space, use the CELLPADDING attribute inside your <TABLE> tag. To add 3 pixels of space on each side of every cell, type <TABLE CELLPADDING=3>.

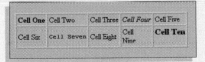

4 You can format text in each individual cell using all of the standard character-level markup codes, such as <B>, <I>, and <STRONG>. You can also include line breaks inside cells using the <BR> tag. Each cell can be formatted independently of the others.

`<TD ALIGN=CENTER VALIGN=CENTER>`

5 To control the alignment of text inside cells, use the ALIGN and VALIGN attributes with the standard commands, such as LEFT, RIGHT, and CENTER. You can set the cell alignment for an entire row by placing these attributes in the <TR> tag. You can even align the contents of each cell individually if you're so inclined. For example, to center text within an individual cell both vertically and horizontally, type <**TD ALIGN–CENTER VALIGN=CENTER**>. Individual cell alignments will override any settings for the row.

Continue to next page ▶

How to Format Tables (Continued)

▶ **7** You can gain even more precise control over the size and appearance of your table using the WIDTH attribute. The WIDTH attribute can be applied to both the entire table as well as individual cells. You can specify an exact width for the table or set the width to be a percentage of the visible screen.

`<TABLE RULES=COLS>`

 You can also control how the internal cell borders are displayed using the RULES attribute. The possible values for RULES are ALL, the default, which displays all of the internal borders; NONE, which disables internal borders; COLS, which places borders only between columns; and ROWS, which places borders only between rows. For example, to place internal cell borders between columns only, you would type <**TABLE ROWS=COLS**>. As with the FRAME attribute, the RULES attribute is new to HTML3 and is not widely supported.

`<TABLE WIDTH=400>`

8 To specify an exact width for your table in pixels, set the WIDTH attribute to an absolute number. For example, to force a table to be exactly 400 pixels wide, type <**TABLE WIDTH=400**>.

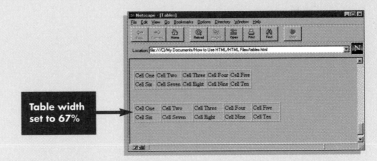

Table width set to 67%

9 You can also set the table width to be relative to the space between the left and right margins of the current window. This means the table will resize along with the Web browser. To set the table width equal to two-thirds of the screen, type <**TABLE WIDTH=66%**>.

Column width set to 50%

`<TABLE FRAME=LHS>`

11 You can specify which sides of the table frame to render using the FRAME attribute inside the <TABLE> tag. The possible choices are VOID (no sides), ABOVE (only the top), BELOW (only the bottom), HSIDES (both top and bottom), LHS (only the left side), RHS (only the right side), VSIDES (both left and right sides), and BORDER (all four sides, the default). For example, to display only the left-hand side of the table frame, you would type <**TABLE FRAME=LHS**>. This attribute is new to HTML3 and is not yet widely supported by Web browsers.

10 You can apply width settings to columns by placing the WIDTH attribute inside a <TH> or <TD> tag. The width can be indicated using absolute or relative numbers. When you use a percentage value in individual cells, the width is relative to the table, not the full screen. For example, to set a column width to one-half the total width of the table, type <**TD WIDTH=50%**>.

TRY IT!

Here's an opportunity to practice all of the skills you've learned in the previous three chapters. Lawn-Birds, Inc. has asked you once again to create an HTML document for their World Wide Web site. This time, they want to create a simple online catalog of their products. They also want to include a form for people to fill out if they'd like to receive a printed version of the catalog in the mail.

You'll get a chance to perform a few advanced graphics tricks as well as put your knowledge of forms and tables to the test. If you get a little stuck along the way, don't worry. You can always refer back to the previous chapters for help.

1

Start Notepad and turn Word Wrap on.

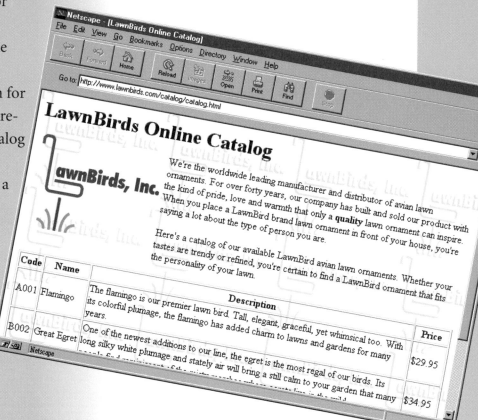

2

Type in the first few lines of your HTML document, pressing Enter after each one.

3

Here's where we'll include a background image, which you learned about in Chapter 9. Since you probably don't have this exact graphic on your system, you can substitute your own image. Remember to use a light-colored, low-contrast image for the background. Make a copy of your image file and name it backlogo.gif.

4

```
<BODY BACKGROUND="backlogo.gif">
```

Type <BODY BACKGROUND="backlogo.gif"> and press Enter.

5

```
<H1>LawnBirds Online Catalog</H1>
```

Insert a headline by typing <H1>LawnBirds Online Catalog</H1>, then press Enter.

6

```
<P>
```

Type <P> to start the first paragraph, then press Enter.

7

```
<IMG SRC="logo.gif" ALT="LawnBirds logo"
ALIGN=LEFT>
```

Now we'll insert the LawnBirds logo. We'll use the version that we created in Chapter 9 with transparency. This will allow the background image to show through. Type <IMG SRC="logo.gif" ALT="LawnBirds logo" ALIGN=LEFT>.

8

```
<IMG SRC="logo.gif" ALT="LawnBirds logo"
ALIGN=LEFT HEIGHT=153 WIDTH=203>
```

Inside the <IMG> tag, type the height and width of the image using the HEIGHT and WIDTH attributes. In our example, the height and width are 153 pixels and 203 pixels, respectively. If you're using a different image, substitute the correct size for each. You can determine the size by opening the image in Paint Shop Pro or another image editing program.

9

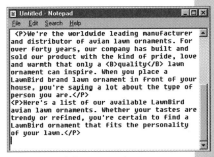

Type in the entire text of the first paragraphs, followed by a </P> tag. Press Enter, and then type in the text of the second paragraph, enclosing it with <P> and </P> tags. Finally, press Enter again.

Continue to next page ▶

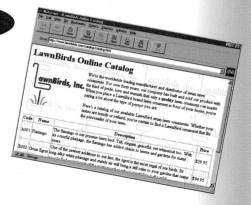

Continue below

10

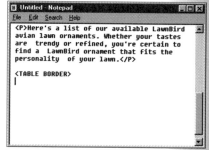

The best way to present the product catalog in HTML is with a table. The columns of the table will be the product code, the product name, a brief description, and the price. To start the table, type **<TABLE BORDER>** and press Enter.

11

<TR>

The first row of cells in the table will contain the column headings. Type <TR> to start the first row, and then press Enter.

12

```
<TH>Code</TH>
<TH>Name</TH>
<TH>Description</TH>
<TH>Price</TH>
```

Type <TH>Code</TH> to specify the contents of the first table heading cell. Then type in the remaining table headings, surrounding each one with a <TH> and </TH> tag pair. To keep things understandable, you may want to type each one on a separate line. When you're finished, press Enter.

13

</TR>

Type </TR> to mark the end of the table row and press Enter.

14

<TR>

Type <TR> to start a new row of cells and press Enter.

15

Now we'll start entering the data for each product in the LawnBirds line. Each item needs to be entered in order using the <TD> and </TD> tag pairs. You can keep all of the <TD> elements on one line, or type each of them on separate lines for readability. To make things easier to follow in this example, we'll put each one on a separate line.

16

<TD>A001</TD>

Type <TD>A001</TD> to mark the product code of the first item in the catalog. Then press Enter.

```
<TD>Flamingo</TD>
```

Type <TD>Flamingo</TD> to enter in the data for the second cell in this row, the product name. Then press Enter.

```
<TD>The flamingo is our premier lawn bird.
Tall, elegant, graceful, yet whimsical too.
With its colorful plumage, the flamingo has
added charm to lawns and gardens for many
years.</TD>
```

Type <TD>, followed by the full product description. If you skipped step 1 and didn't turn on Word Wrap, you'll probably want to turn it on now. When you're finished typing in the description, type </TD> to close the cell. Then press Enter.

```
<TD>$29.95</TD>
```

Type <TD>$29.95</TD> to enter the contents of the final cell in this row, the price. Then press Enter.

```
</TR>
<TR>
```

Type </TR> to mark the end of this table row, then press Enter. Type <TR> to mark the beginning of the next row, and press Enter again.

Code	Name	Description	Price
A001	Flamingo	The flamingo is our premier lawn bird. Tall, elegant, graceful, yet whimsical too. With its colorful plumage, the flamingo has added charm to lawns and gardens for many years.	$29.95
B002	Great Egret	One of the newest additions to our line, the egret is the most regal of our birds. Its long silky white plumage and stately air will bring a still calm to your garden that many people find reminiscent of the misty marshes where egrets live in the wild.	$34.95
C003	Ostrich	What could be more fun than waking up and looking out your bedroom window to see our playful and exciting ostrich cavorting on your lawn? This new addition to our line brings a smile and a giggle to the LawnBirds family.	$24.95
D004	Condor	Fill your lawn with a sense of awe and wonderment with our breathtaking Condor. Boasting an impressive wingspan of 25 feet, the Condor makes its presence known in your neighborhood. Custom-built by noted lawn ornament designer Erik Kokkonen, each Condor is numbered and engraved with Erik's signature mark.	$189.95

Repeat the above steps for each row of data. Remember that each row must begin with a <TR> tag and end with a </TR> tag. Each cell begins with a <TD> and ends with a </TD>.

```
</TABLE>
```

When you're finished entering the data for all the cells, type </TABLE> and press Enter.

```
<HR>
```

Now we'll create a simple online form for readers to fill out if they'd like to receive a printed version of the catalog in the mail. First, we'll separate the form from the rest of the document by placing a horizontal rule. Type <HR> and then press Enter.

```
<P>If you'd like to receive a FREE printed
version of the LawnBirds catalog, please
fill out the form below and press the
'Submit Query' button to send your address
to us via EMail. Thank you.</P>
```

Before you create the form, place an introductory paragraph in the document explaining what the form is for. Type <P>, followed by the text of the paragraph. Then type </P> and press Enter.

Continue to next page ▶

TRY IT!

Continue
below

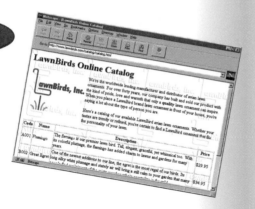

25

```
<FORM METHOD=POST>
```

Now type **<FORM METHOD=POST>**
to start creating the form.

26

```
ACTION="mailto:catalog@lawnbirds.com">
```

Because this is a very simple request form, we'll
just have the results sent to an e-mail address at
LawnBirds. Inside the <FORM> tag, type
ACTION="mailto:catalog@ lawnbirds.com".

27

Move the cursor to the end of the <FORM>
tag and press Enter.

28

```
<P>Last Name:
```

Type **<P>** to start a paragraph, and
then type **Last Name:**. This is the label
for your first input field.

29

```
<P>Last Name: <INPUT NAME="lastname"
TYPE=text WIDTH=20>
<BR>
```

Type **<INPUT NAME="lastname"
TYPE=text WIDTII=20>** to place the
actual input field. This creates a single-
line text field with a maximum length
of 20 characters. Now type **
** to
place a line break and press Enter.

30

```
First Name: <INPUT NAME="firstname"
TYPE=text WIDTH=12>
<BR>
```

Type **First
Name:** followed by **<INPUT
NAME="firstname" TYPE=text
WIDTH=12>** to place the second
input field. Again, type **
** on
the next line and press Enter.

31

```
Address: <INPUT NAME="address1"
TYPE=text WIDTH=40>
<BR>
```

Type **Address:** followed by **<INPUT
NAME="address1" TYPE=text
WIDTH=40>** to create the first line of
the address field. Then type **
** and
press Enter.

32

```
<INPUT NAME="address2" TYPE=text WIDTH=40>
<BR>
```

Type **<INPUT NAME="address2"
TYPE=text WIDTH=40>** to create the
second line of the address field. Then
type **
** on the next line and press
Enter.

```
City:<INPUT NAME="city" TYPE=text WIDTH=20>
State:<INPUT NAME="state" TYPE=text WIDTH=2>
Zip:<INPUT NAME="zip" TYPE=text WIDTH=5>
```

To create the
final line of input, which contains the city,
state, and zip code information, type **City:**
followed by **<INPUT NAME="city"
TYPE=text WIDTH=20>** to create an
input field for the city. Then type **State:**
followed by **<INPUT NAME="state"
TYPE=text WIDTH=2>**. Finally, type **Zip:**
followed by **<INPUT NAME="zip"
TYPE=text WIDTH=5>**.

```
<BR>
<INPUT NAME="submit" TYPE=submit>
```

Type **
** to force a line break. Press
Enter and then type **<INPUT
NAME="submit" TYPE=submit>** to
create the Submit button.

```
<INPUT NAME="reset" TYPE=reset>
```

Type **<INPUT NAME="reset"
TYPE=reset>** to create the Reset
button, which will clear all of the
input fields. Then type **</P>** to close
the paragraph, and press Enter.

```
</FORM>
```

Type **</FORM>** to close the form and
then press Enter.

```
</BODY>
```

Type **</BODY>** to close the body
section and then press Enter.

```
</HTML>
```

Type **</HTML>** to mark the end of the
HTML document.

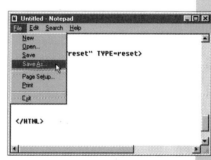

Select Save
As from the
File menu
and save your
document. In
this example,
we'll name
the file catalog.html.

CHAPTER 12

Creating Clickable Images

 If you've experimented with images and links, which you learned about in previous chapters, you've probably already discovered that you can use an image to create a hyperlink to another HTML document. But what about using a single image to link to several different documents? It can be done using clickable images, also known as *image maps*.

When you use a clickable image map, the user clicks on a part of the image. The server records the coordinates of the part that was clicked, and your image map directs the server to process a hyperlink accordingly.

You've probably seen image maps on a lot of Web sites that you have visited. Image maps are an excellent way to visually present links in an intuitive and friendly fashion. Creating your own image maps isn't hard to do, but it requires some careful preparation. In this chapter you'll learn how to create and prepare image maps for use with your own HTML documents.

How to Create a Clickable Image

The first part of building a clickable image map is creating the image to be used. Your image should be simple and easy to understand, with clearly delineated sections.

▶ **1** Create your clickable image using Paint Shop Pro or another image editing program that can save files in GIF or JPEG format. In this example, we'll use a button bar.

8 Once you've finished creating or editing your image, save it in GIF or JPEG format.

7 Circles are defined by finding the coordinates of the circle's center and measuring the radius in pixels.

2 When creating an image map, make the actual image as simple to understand as possible. You should always try to place text in the image to help your readers understand which sections of the image to click. Photographs and other images that lack clearly defined sections are usually poor choices for image maps.

3 Plan out in advance the different sections of your image map and where their associated links will point. Making substantial changes to images is always time-consuming and difficult, so you'll want to account for all the possibilities before you create your image.

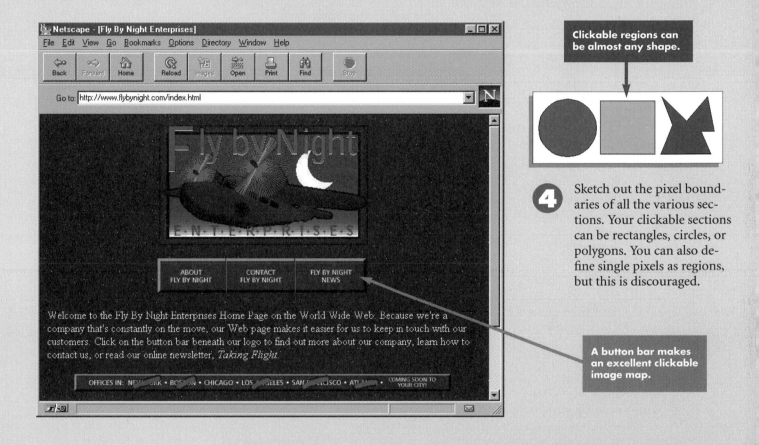

Clickable regions can be almost any shape.

4 Sketch out the pixel boundaries of all the various sections. Your clickable sections can be rectangles, circles, or polygons. You can also define single pixels as regions, but this is discouraged.

A button bar makes an excellent clickable image map.

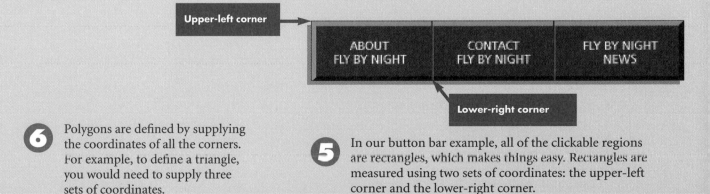

Upper-left corner

Lower-right corner

6 Polygons are defined by supplying the coordinates of all the corners. For example, to define a triangle, you would need to supply three sets of coordinates.

5 In our button bar example, all of the clickable regions are rectangles, which makes things easy. Rectangles are measured using two sets of coordinates: the upper-left corner and the lower-right corner.

How to Create a Map File

The second part of building a clickable image map is creating the map file. This text file contains a list of coordinates that form the map regions. Each clickable region has an associated hyperlink. The Web server reads the map file to match the coordinates of the pixel that was clicked by the user, and then determines which hyperlink to send the user to.

You can find the latest version of Map This! by pointing your Web browser to http://galadriel.ecaetc.ohio-state.edu/tc/mt.

▶ **1** Start Map This! and select New from the File menu. You'll be prompted to locate an image to use for the map. Open your existing GIF or JPEG file.

OK

9 Click on the OK button. Then, choose a file name for your map file. Your file should have the extension **.map**. Click on the Save button when you're finished.

8 Repeat steps 2–5 until all of the clickable regions in your image have been defined and associated with links. The last item in the Info dialog box is the map file format. Different Web servers recognize different image map file formats. The default format is NCSA, which is the most widely used. You should check with your server administrator to see which format you need to select.

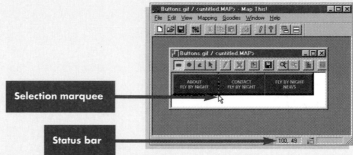

2 Select the appropriate icon shape from the toolbar for the type of clickable region you want to define.

Selection marquee

Status bar

3 Click and drag the selection marquee across the region. The status bar will display exact coordinate information.

4 Click on the arrow icon in the toolbar to select an existing area. Then double-click on the region you just defined.

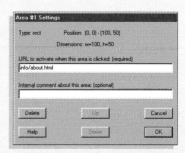

5 In the Area Settings dialog box, specify the URL of the item that this region should link to. For example, to link to an HTML document named *about.html* in a subdirectory called *info/*, type **info/about.html**. For more information on URLs and links, refer back to Chapter 6.

7 When you're finished defining clickable regions, choose Save As from the File menu. You'll be prompted to fill out the Info dialog box. Type in a title for your Map file and put your name in the Author field. The default URL is used when the user clicks on a part of the image that is not defined by one of your regions. You should also supply a brief description of what your map file does.

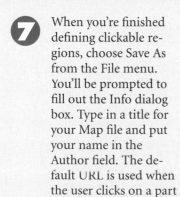

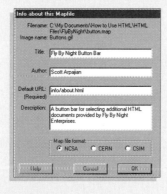

6 Repeat steps 2–5 until all of the clickable regions in your image have been defined and associated with links.

How to Define an Image Map in HTML

The last thing you need to do to create an image map is to place it on your Web server and place a reference to it in your HTML document.

An image map works just like a CGI script, and usually belongs in the same directory as scripts on your server. Consult your Web server administrator for details on how to upload your completed map file to the appropriate directory. The actual image can be placed anywhere you like, although it's generally a good idea to place it in the same directory as your HTML document.

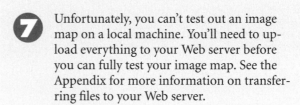

```
<A HREF="cgi-bin/button.map">
```

▶ **1** Open your HTML document in Notepad, and position the cursor where you'd like to place the image map. An image map is placed into HTML as a hyperlink. Type **<A HREF="">** and insert the name of your map file inside the quotation marks. For example, if your map file is named buttons.map and is located in the cgi-bin directory on your server, you would type **<A HREF="cgi-bin/buttons.map">**.

7 Unfortunately, you can't test out an image map on a local machine. You'll need to upload everything to your Web server before you can fully test your image map. See the Appendix for more information on transferring files to your Web server.

6 Save the edited HTML file by selecting Save from the File menu in Notepad.

TIP SHEET

▸ For more information on hyperlinks, refer back to Chapter 6.

▸ Turning images into hyperlinks usually causes a blue border to be displayed around the image. To turn the border off, type BORDER=0 inside the **<IMG>** tag.

2 Some Web servers handle image maps differently than normal CGI scripts. Be sure to check with your server administrator for exact instructions on how to link to your image map.

```
<IMG SRC="buttons.gif" ISMAP>
```

3 Now you need to include a reference to the actual image, with one important attribute specified. Image map graphics need to include the attribute ISMAP inside the <IMG> tag. For example, to include the image buttons.gif as an image map graphic, type <IMG SRC="buttons.gif" ISMAP>.

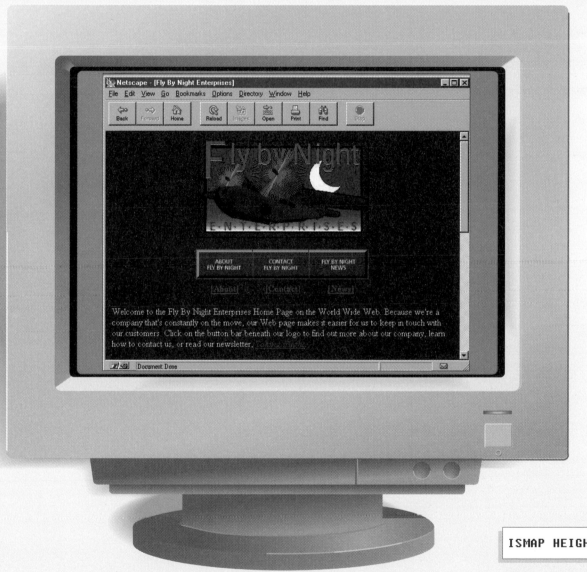

```
ISMAP HEIGHT=50 WIDTH=305>
```

4 You should also specify the height and width of your image inside the <IMG> tag using the HEIGHT and WIDTH attributes.

```
</A>
```

5 Close your link by typing </A>.

CHAPTER 13

Using the Netscape Extensions

When the original version of Netscape was introduced, it contained a number of extensions to the HTML language. These extensions quickly became popular with both Web surfers and Web designers because they added functionality to the Web that standard HTML could not provide. Because of Netscape's popularity, many of these extensions are in widespread use, and have become the de facto standard on the Web.

Many of the original Netscape extensions have since been incorporated into the HTML3 standard. However, following its own precedent, Netscape 2.0 introduces some additional extensions that may prove to be just as popular.

In this chapter, you'll learn about a few of the original Netscape extensions that have not been incorporated into the official HTML3 specification, as well as the new proposed extensions.

How to Use Netscape's Formatting Extensions

The most popular of the original Netscape extensions were the ones used to make formatting text in HTML more flexible. Many of the original extensions have since been incorporated into the HTML3 standard, and are therefore discussed elsewhere in this book. However, some formatting extensions still remain unofficial, and many are in widespread use. You may choose to incorporate these extensions into your HTML document, but keep in mind that if you do, many non-Netscape browsers will not recognize the formatting you have specified.

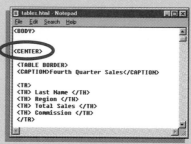

1 One of the most commonly used Netscape Extensions is the <CENTER> tag. Although using the ALIGN=CENTER attribute is generally preferred, there are some situations where you'll want to center items such as tables on the page. To use the <CENTER> tag, open an existing HTML document in Notepad and type <**CENTER**> at the point where you'd like the centering to begin.

```
<BASEFONT SIZE=5>
```

6 You can change the value of the base font size using the <BASEFONT> tag. For example, to change the default font size from 3 to 5, type <BASEFONT SIZE=5>.

TIP SHEET

▶ **Try to use the ALIGN=CENTER attribute instead of <CENTER> whenever possible. In HTML3, most block elements—such as paragraphs, tables, and images—can be centered in your HTML document using the ALIGN attribute, which is "official" HTML.**

▶ **One of the cardinal sins of the <BLINK> tag is overusing it. In fact, most experienced Web surfers prefer that you don't use it at all. If you feel that you must use the <BLINK> tag in your documents, please don't tell anyone that you read about it in this book. I'll deny everything.**

▶ **The <FONT> tag should not be used in place of headline tags, such as <H1>. Not all browsers support the <FONT> tag; they will display <FONT> formatted text in the default size. You should continue to use headline tags when the text absolutely must appear in a headline style.**

```
tables.html - Notepad
File  Edit  Search  Help
<TD>Midwest</TD>
<TD>$285,300</TD>
<TD>$14,265</TD>
</TR>
</TABLE>

</CENTER>


<H2>Sales Information</H2>

<TABLE>
```

2 Type </CENTER> at the point where you'd like the centering to end. When this HTML document is viewed by a Netscape browser, or any other browser that supports the <CENTER> tag, everything that falls between the <CENTER> and </CENTER> tags will appear centered in the browser. This includes paragraphs, headlines, images and tables.

```
<BLINK>This text will blink.</BLINK>
```

3 You can also create blinking text. This is a controversial Netscape tag, because the effect it creates is considered annoying by many people. Try it out yourself and make your own decision. To make any text blink, surround it with **<BLINK>** and **</BLINK>** tags.

```
<FONT SIZE=5>This text is bigger than
the rest.</FONT>
```

4 The Netscape extensions also give you greater control over the size of fonts as they appear in the browser. You can specify an absolute font size by typing <FONT SIZE= followed by a number from 1 to 7. The default font size is 3. The new font size will stay in effect until a </FONT> tag appears. For example, to make text in a paragraph appear slightly larger than normal, type **<FONT SIZE=5>This text is bigger than the rest.</FONT>**.

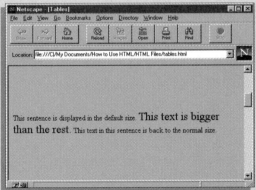

5 Instead of using absolute font sizes, you can specify font size relative to a base font value using the + and - signs in front of a value. The default base font size is 3. For example, to achieve the same effect in the previous step using relative font sizes, you would type **<FONT SIZE=+2>This text is bigger than the rest.</FONT>**.

How to Extend Your Lists with Netscape

In Chapter 7, you learned how to use lists in HTML to present compact, concise information. Netscape allows you to extend lists considerably. You can change the appearance of bullets in unordered lists and change the numbering style of ordered lists. You can even switch between numbering styles in the middle of a list.

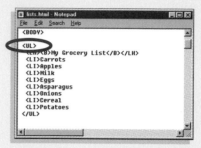

1 You can change the appearance of the bullets used in an unordered list. First, open the HTML document containing your list and look for the <UL> tag, which marks the beginning of the list.

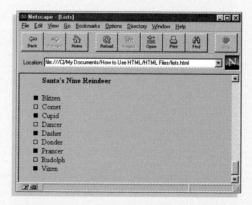

6 Netscape's extensions allow you to use the TYPE and VALUE attributes in individual <LI> line item tags. For example, in an unordered list, you could alternate the bullet style for each item by specifying a bullet type in each <LI> tag.

TIP SHEET

▶ For more information on lists in HTML, refer back to Chapter 7.

▶ Remember that these extensions are only recognized by Netscape browsers. Users with other browsers will not see the formatting changes you have made to your lists.

2 Add the attribute **TYPE=** to the <UL> tag, followed by either **disc**, **square**, or **circle** to indicate the type of bullet used. For example, to make the bullets in your list appear as squares, you would type <UL TYPE=**square**>.

3 You can also change the numbering scheme for ordered lists. By default, ordered lists start at 1, and the number increases incrementally by one for each list item. To change the type of numbering used, open your HTML document and locate the <OL> tag, which marks the beginning of the ordered list.

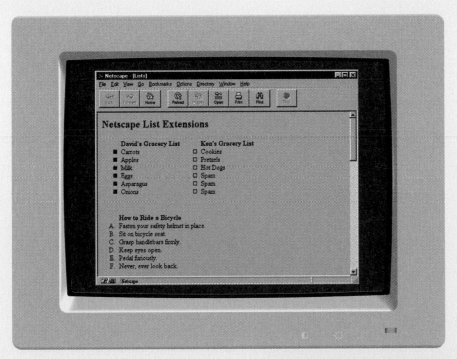

<OL TYPE=A>

4 To change the numbering scheme of your list to capital letters (A,B,C, and so on), add the attribute **TYPE=A** to the <OL> tag. The items in your list will use capital letters instead of numbers in front of each list item.

5 You can also use lowercase letters by typing **TYPE=a** inside the <OL> tag. Typing **TYPE=I** uses uppercase Roman numerals (I,II,III) as the numbering scheme. Finally, you can use lowercase Roman numerals by typing **TYPE=i** inside the <OL> tag.

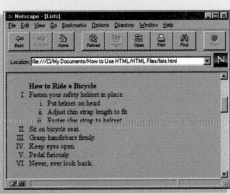

How to Extend Horizontal Rules

In Chapter 5, you learned how to create a horizontal rule in HTML. Horizontal rules, which are specified with an <HR> tag, are useful for breaking apart sections of your HTML document. Netscape supports a number of useful extensions to the <HR> tag, giving you greater control over the format of horizontal rules in your documents.

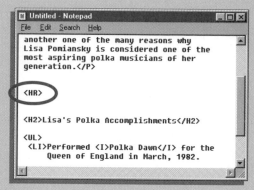

1 Open the HTML document containing the horizontal rule, and locate the <HR> tag.

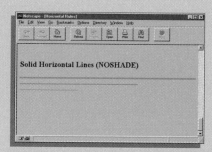

6 Netscape also allows you to display your horizontal rule as a solid line instead of the normal beveled "3-D" bar. To turn off the fancy shading effects for the horizontal rule, add the NOSHADE attribute to your <HR> tag. For example, to create a solid horizontal rule that is 5 pixels thick, you would type <HR SIZE=5 NOSHADE>.

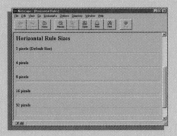

2 You can change the thickness of the horizontal rule by using the SIZE attribute, measured in pixels. The default size is 2 pixels. For example, to change the width of the horizontal tag to 8 pixels, you would type <HR SIZE=8>.

3 By default, a horizontal rule stretches across the entire width of the browser window. You can change the width of any horizontal rule using the WIDTH attribute inside the <HR> tag. To specify an exact width, indicate the number of pixels. For example, to set the width of a horizontal rule to 200 pixels, type <HR WIDTH=200>.

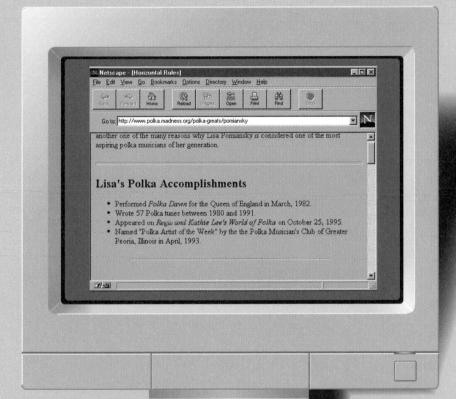

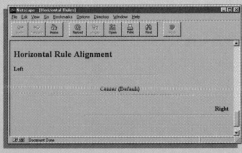

4 You can also define the width of a horizontal rule as a percentage of the visible screen. For example, to set the width of the horizontal rule to be one-half of the screen, type <HR WIDTH=50%>.

5 If you've changed the width of a horizontal rule to be less than the default full-screen size, you can also specify how the horizontal rule is aligned on the page. By default, horizontal rules are centered on the page, but by adding the ALIGN attribute to the <HR> tag, you can align the rules to the left or right margin. For example, to create a horizontal rule that is one-third the width of the visible screen and is aligned with the left margin, you would type <HR WIDTH=33% ALIGN=LEFT>.

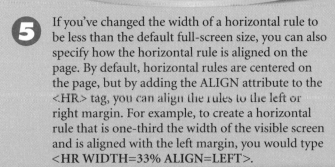

How to Use Client-Side Image Maps

In Chapter 12, you learned how to create clickable image maps using CGI and server-based map files. Although this process is popular, there are many drawbacks. First, normal image maps require increased interaction with the server. Whenever the user clicks on part of the image, the server must be contacted to determine where that portion of the image links to. This can slow things down considerably, depending on where the server is in relation to the user and the amount of user traffic on that server at any given time. Also, normal image maps cannot be used for HTML documents that are accessed locally or on a LAN. They only work via the HTTP protocol on the World Wide Web. Finally, users do not receive visual feedback on the link destination with image maps as they do with normal hypertext links.

Netscape 2.0 now supports client-side image maps. The crucial difference is that all the link and region instructions—the map files—are now stored directly in the HTML document. The browser takes care of all the work locally. Client-side image maps are only supported by a few browsers. Fortunately, there's a way to set up your image maps with both a client-side and a normal server version, so that your image maps will work with all browsers.

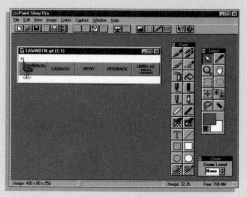

1 Select the graphic to be used as the image map. As with normal image maps, the graphic should be clearly divided into easily distinguishable regions.

```
<MAP NAME="buttonbar">
<AREA SHAPE="RECT">
```

7 The <AREA> tag has three required attributes. The first is the SHAPE attribute. Currently, the only supported shape in client-side image maps is the rectangle. To define a rectangle, type **SHAPE="RECT"** inside the <AREA> tag.

```
<MAP NAME="buttonbar">
<AREA>
```

6 Each clickable region is defined using an <AREA> tag. If you define two regions that overlap, Netscape will use the first region specified when determining which link to use. To define the first region in your map, type <**AREA**>.

2 Open the HTML document in which you'd like to place the client-side image map, and place the cursor at the point in the document where you'd like the image map to be displayed.

```
<IMG SRC="lawnbutn.gif">
```

3 Place the image using the standard image tag. For example, to insert an image named lawnbutn.gif, type <IMG SRC="lawnbutn.gif">.

```
<IMG SRC="lawnbutn.gif" USEMAP="#buttonbar">

<MAP NAME="buttonbar">
```

```
<IMG SRC="lawnbutn.gif" USEMAP="#buttonbar">
```

5 Now you'll create the actual map inside your HTML document using the <MAP> tag. On a new line, type <MAP NAME="buttonbar"> and press Enter.

4 Inside the <IMG> tag, add the USEMAP= attribute, followed by the name of a map enclosed by quotes and prefaced with a pound sign (#). The name of the map can be anything you like. You'll create the actual map in the next step. For example, to point to a map named *buttonbar*, type USEMAP="#buttonbar" inside the <IMG> tag.

Continue to next page ▶

How to Use Client-Side Image Maps (Continued)

```
<MAP NAME="buttonbar">
<AREA SHAPE="RECT" COORDS="0,0,79,39">
```

▶ **8** The next step is to define the coordinates of your rectangle. Determine the x and y coordinates of the upper-left and lower-right corners of your rectangle and type them in using the COORDS= attribute. For example, if your rectangle started at the upper-left corner of the image (coordinates 0,0) and extended 80 pixels wide and 40 pixels down, you would type **COORDS="0,0,79,39"** inside the <AREA> tag.

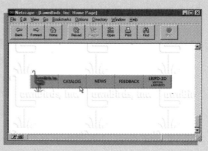

15 Save your HTML document and test the client-side image map with your Netscape browser.

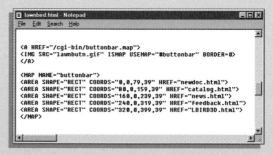

14 To make your image map work as a server-side map, you will also need to enclose it with an anchor element that links to a map file stored on the server. Obviously, you will also need to create the map file itself. Refer back to Chapter 12 for instructions on creating a server-based image map. The accompanying screen shot shows what a dual image map reference might look like.

TIP SHEET

▶ **For more information on clickable image maps, refer back to Chapter 12.**

```
<MAP NAME="buttonbar">
<AREA SHAPE="RECT" COORDS="0,0,79,39" HREF="newdoc.html">
```

9 Now you need to provide the URL of the link that is activated when the user clicks in this region. Inside the <AREA> tag, type **HREF=**, followed by the name of the URL in quotation marks. You can use either a full URL or a relative URL. For example, to link to another HTML document in the same directory as the active document, type **HREF="newdoc.html"**.

10 In some cases, you might want to define a clickable region with no hyperlink. Instead of using the HREF attribute, type **NOHREF**. When a user clicks on this region, no action will be performed.

```
<MAP NAME="buttonbar">
<AREA SHAPE="RECT" COORDS="0,0,79,39" HREF="newdoc.html">
<AREA SHAPE="RECT" COORDS="80,0,159,39" HREF="catalog.html">
<AREA SHAPE="RECT" COORDS="160,0,239,39" HREF="news.html">
<AREA SHAPE="RECT" COORDS="240,0,319,39" HREF="feedback.html">
<AREA SHAPE="RECT" COORDS="320,0,399,39" HREF="LBIRD3D.html">
```

11 Create <AREA> tags for each of the remaining clickable regions you want to define.

```
<IMG SRC="lawnbutn.gif" ISMAP USEMAP="#button
```

13 Your client-side image map will now work with Netscape browsers. However, if you want your image map to work with other browsers, you'll need to make it function as a normal image map as well. The first step is to add the ISMAP attribute to the IMG tag. Netscape browsers will use the map specified in the USEMAP attribute. Other browsers will ignore USEMAP and use ISMAP instead, treating this image as a server-based clickable image map.

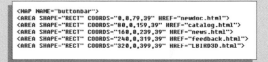

```
</MAP>
```

12 Type </MAP> to finish the image map definition.

Impressed with your previous
work, LawnBirds, Inc. has asked
you to update their World Wide
Web home page once again. They'd
like you to include a graphical button bar menu at the bottom of each
of their HTML documents. Clicking
on the different sections of this button will load the various Web pages
in the LawnBirds Web site.

Here's a chance to practice your
image map skills. You'll create two
image maps in this exercise: a normal server-based image map and a
client-side image map, which will
take advantage of the Netscape
extensions.

Launch Notepad
and open the
lawnbirds.html
file that you
saved at the end
of the second Try It! section.

The current file has some information that we no longer need. In the third Try It! sec-

tion, you created a full catalog of LawnBirds products, so it's no longer necessary to list the products on the main LawnBirds page. Delete the entire second paragraph, as well as the definition list containing the product descriptions. We'll leave the list of contact information on the main page.

Save the file in Notepad.

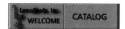

Now we'll work on the button bar image that visitors to the LawnBirds Web page will use to navigate around the site. In this example, we've already created a button bar called lawnbar.gif.

Since you don't have this image on your system, you'll need to create one using Paint Shop Pro or another image editing program. A simple rectangle divided into two sections will work just fine. When you're finished creating your image, save it as lawnbar.gif.

Launch Map This! and choose New from the File menu.

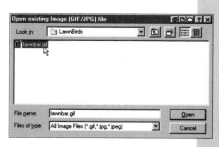

Map This! will prompt you to open an image file. Locate lawn-bar.gif and open it.

Click on the rectangle tool from the toolbar.

Drag the selection marquee over the area of the first button on your bar.

Continue to next page ▶

TRY IT!

Continue
below

10

Drag the
selection
marquee over the area of the second
button on your bar.

11

Click on the arrow tool from the toolbar.

12

Place the cur-
sor over the
first selection
area and
double-click.
In the Area
#1 Settings
dialog box,
type **lawn-

bird.html** as the URL to activate when this
area is clicked. That means that clicking on
this button will load the LawnBirds, Inc.
main page. When you're finished, click on
the OK button.

13

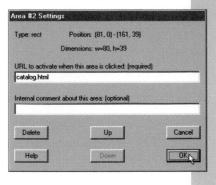

Place the cur-
sor over the
second selec-
tion area and
double-click.
In the Area
#2 Settings
dialog box,
type **cata-

log.html** as the URL to activate when this area
is clicked. This will load the LawnBirds, Inc.
catalog page that you created in the previous
Try It! section. When you're finished, click on
the OK button.

14

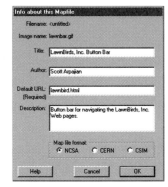

Choose Save
As from the
File menu. In
the Title
box, type
**LawnBirds,
Inc. Button
Bar**. Type in
your name in
the Author field. In the default URL field,
type **lawnbird.html**. You can also type in a
description of your map file.

15

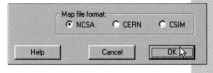

Choose the
map file for-
mat for your server. If you're not sure which
format to use, check with your Web server administrator. In this example, we'll choose NCSA,
which is the default. Once you've selected the
map file format, click on the OK button.

Save the file as **lawnbar.map**.

Close Map This! and return to Notepad. If you previously closed Notepad, launch it again and open lawnbird.html.

Place the cursor near the bottom of the file, right above the closing </BODY> tag, but after the closing </UL> tag from the list of contact information.

Type <A HREF="cgi-bin/lawnbar.map"> and press Enter. If your map files are stored in a directory other than cgi-bin, you'll need to change the path name in the above URL. Check with your Web server administrator for details on where to place image map files.

```
</UL>

<A HREF="cgi-bin/lawnbar.map">
|
```

```
<A HREF="cgi-bin/lawnbar.map">
<IMG SRC="lawnbar.gif" ALIGN=BOTTOM ISMAP
USEMAP="#lawnbar">
|
```

Type <IMG SRC="lawnbar.gif" ALIGN=BOTTOM ISMAP USEMAP="#lawnbar"> and press Enter. This instructs the Web browser to load the button bar image and align any text along its bottom. The ISMAP attribute lets the browser know that this graphic is part of an image map. Finally, the USEMAP attribute allows Netscape browsers to use a client-side image map instead of the server-based one. You'll create the client-side image map in a few moments.

```
<IMG SRC="lawnbar.gif" ISMAP
USEMAP="#lawnbar" ALIGN=BOTTOM>
</A>
|
```

Type </A> to close the link to the server-based image map and press Enter.

```
<MAP NAME="lawnbar">
|
```

Now we'll create the client-side image map, which is contained inside the actual HTML document. Type <MAP NAME="lawnbar"> and press Enter.

```
<MAP NAME="lawnbar">
<AREA SHAPE="RECT" COORDS="0,0,79,39"
HREF="lawnbird.html">
|
```

Type <AREA SHAPE="RECT" COORDS="0,0,79,39" HREF="lawnbird.html">. This defines a rectangle that is 80 pixels wide and 40 pixels high that links to lawnbird.html. That happens to be the same file you're working in right now, so pressing on this button would simply reload the current page. Press Enter when you're finished.

Continue to next page ►

Continue
below

```
<AREA SHAPE="RECT" COORDS="81,0,160,39"
HREF="catalog.html">
|
```

Type **<AREA SHAPE="RECT" COORDS= "81,0,160,39" HREF="catalog.html">**. This defines your second button and establishes a link to the document catalog.html. Press Enter when you're finished.

```
<AREA SHAPE="RECT" COORDS="81,0,160,39"
HREF="catalog.html">
</MAP>
|
```

Type **</MAP>** to finish the client-side image map, and press Enter.

Now you have a functioning button bar that works both as a server-based and a client-side image map. However, you should consider how to handle users with browsers that do not handle images at all. To accommodate those users, we'll create text-only hyperlinks and place them below the button bar image map.

```
<P><A HREF="lawnbird.html">Welcome Page</A>
|
```

Type **<P>** to start a new paragraph. Then type **<A HREF="lawnbird.html">Welcome Page</A>** and press Enter. This creates a simple text-only link that points to the main LawnBirds, Inc. page.

```
<P><A HREF="lawnbird.html">Welcome Page</A>
| <A HREF="catalog.html">Catalog</A></P>|
```

Type the "pipe symbol," which is the vertical bar that usually appears above the backward slash key on your keyboard. The pipe symbol is commonly used as a divider for text-only browsers. Then type **<A HREF="catalog.html" >Catalog</A></P>** and then press Enter. This creates a link to the LawnBirds, Inc. catalog and closes the paragraph.

Save your file in Notepad.

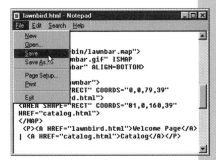

Now we need to copy the button bar image map to the catalog.html file. This will allow users to switch between the two HTML documents by clicking on the two buttons. Rather than typing everything in again, we'll use the cut and paste capabilities of Windows to copy everything from one file to another.

Select everything from **<A HREF="cgi-bin/lawn-bar.map">** to the last line you typed.

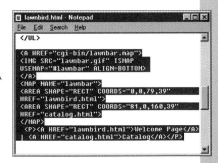

32 Choose Copy from the Edit menu, or press Ctrl+C to copy the text you just selected to the Windows Clipboard.

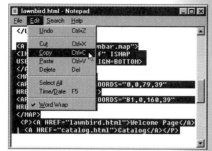

33 Now open catalog.html in Notepad.

34 Place the cursor at the bottom of the document, right before the closing </BODY> tag.

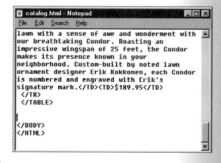

35 Choose Paste from the Edit menu, or press Ctrl+V. This will paste a copy of all the image map code into catalog.html.

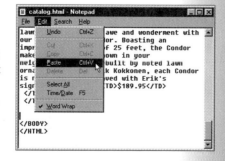

36 Choose Save from the File menu to save the modified catalog.html file.

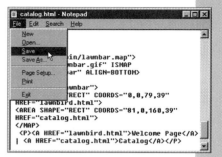

37 Make sure both lawnbird.html and catalog.html are in the same folder. The hyperlinks you created in the image map assume that these files are located in the same folder, and the links won't work if they are not.

38 Launch your Web browser, and open the lawnbird.html file.

39 If your Web browser supports client-side image maps, try clicking on the button bar. Clicking on the

Welcome button will reload the current document. Clicking on the Catalog button will load the LawnBirds, Inc. Catalog. Click on the button bar at the bottom of that document to return to the main page. Congratulations, you've created a working image map!

CHAPTER 14

Using Netscape Frames

 One of the most significant developments in Netscape extensions to HTML3 is the introduction of frames. Using frames gives you the power to divide the reader's browser window into multiple panes. You can display different HTML documents in each. More importantly, you can control the display of one frame from another.

This allows you to create banners, menus, and button bars that don't scroll off the page. For example, you could create a frame for your company logo at the top of the page and a frame for a button bar for navigation at the bottom. A third frame in the middle of the page would display the actual contents of the HTML documents. The top and bottom frames would never disappear from view.

There are a lot of possibilities with frames, and in this chapter, you'll learn the basics of using frames with Netscape browsers. Understanding how to use frames requires some new ways of thinking about HTML documents. If things start to get a little confusing, be patient and take time to reread each section. With a little practice, you'll be working wonders with HTML and frames.

There's one important thing to keep in mind—currently frames are only supported by Netscape 2.0. Although other browsers will most likely add support for frames in the future, you'll need Netscape 2.0 if you want to create frames now.

How to Create Frame Documents

The first thing to understand about frames is that they use an entirely new kind of HTML document, called a frame document. Frame documents control the layout and appearance of the frames. Frame documents don't contain any other HTML content.

Once you've built your frame document, you can fill the frames with regular HTML documents. But before we get too far ahead of ourselves, let's concentrate on creating a very simple set of frames.

In this section, we'll create an empty frame document. Actually, the frame document is not empty. It will only *appear* empty when viewed with the browser, because we won't be putting any regular HTML documents inside. This section will give you a chance to understand how frame layout works.

1 Open a new document in Notepad, and type in <HTML>. Press Enter, then type in <HEAD>. Press Enter again.

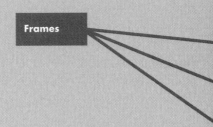

9 You have now created a very simple frame document that contains three empty frames. If this document were viewed in Netscape, it would look exactly like the document shown in the monitor in the center of the page. It may not look like much right now, but in the next section, you'll learn how to make your frames come alive.

TIP SHEET

► You can divide the window into vertical frames by using **COLS** in place of **ROWS** in the **<FRAMESET>** tag.

► You can nest one **<FRAMESET>** tag inside of another to create more complex frame layouts. You'll learn more about extending frame layouts later in this chapter.

8 Save your document in Notepad as myframe.html.

```
<HTML>
<HEAD>
<TITLE>My First Frame Document</TITLE>
</HEAD>
|
```

2 Type <TITLE>My First Frame Document</TITLE>, then press Enter. On the next line, type </HEAD> and press Enter one more time.

3 So far, this looks just like a normal HTML document. Here's where things get different, though. Instead of typing <BODY>, type <FRAMESET>. The <FRAMESET> tag instructs Netscape that this is a frame layout document.

```
</HEAD>
<FRAMESET>|
```

```
</HEAD>
<FRAMESET ROWS="*,*,*">
```

4 Place the cursor inside the <FRAMESET> tag and type ROWS="*,*,*". This creates three horizontal frames of equal relative height. The asterisk character instructs the browser to give the frame all the remaining space in the window. Because there are three asterisks, Netscape will give each frame one-third of the available space.

```
<FRAMESET ROWS="*,*,*">
  <FRAME NAME="frame1" SRC="blank.html">
```

5 On the next line, type <FRAME NAME=frame1 SRC="blank.html">. This assigns the name *frame1* to the first frame in your document. The SRC attribute tells the browser to display the HTML document named blank.html in this frame. Normally, you would place a real HTML document in the SRC attribute. For this example, we'll just use blank.html, a made-up file name that doesn't really exist. Press Enter when you're finished.

```
<FRAME NAME="frame3" SRC="blank.html">
</FRAMESET>
</HTML>|
```

7 Type <FRAMESET> and press Enter. Then type </HTML>.

```
<FRAME NAME="frame2" SRC="blank.html">
<FRAME NAME="frame3" SRC="blank.html">
```

6 Type <FRAME NAME=frame2 SRC="blank.html"> and then press Enter. On the next line, type <FRAME NAME=frame3 SRC="blank.html"> and press Enter again. Now we've created three empty named frames.

Netscape - [My First Frame Document]

File Edit View Go Bookmarks Options Directory Window Help

Back | Forward | Home | Reload | Images | Open | Print | Find | Stop

Document: Done

How to Use Targets in Frames

Now that you've created a frame document, you're ready to start filling those frames with HTML content. In this section you'll learn how to place HTML documents in frames. More importantly, you'll learn how to update frames with new documents, including how to update the contents of one frame from another.

▶ **1** Frames are updated using targets. *Targets* are simply hyperlink tag extensions that contain a frame name. Targets specify which frame the hyperlink should update.

```
<A HREF="a.html" TARGET="frame2">A</A>
<A HREF="b.html" TARGET="frame2">B</A>
<A HREF="c.html" TARGET="frame2">C</A>
```

9 Type in all three hyperlinks again, only this time, change the target to *frame2*. This will instruct the browser to load the documents into the middle frame.

```
<BR>
Middle Frame:
```

8 Type <BR> to force a line break and press enter. Then type **Middle Frame:** and press Enter again.

2 Before we go any further, we'll need to create a few HTML documents that contain hyperlinks using targets. Launch Notepad and open a new document. Then type <HTML> and press Enter.

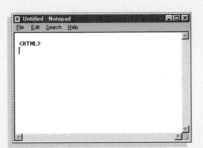

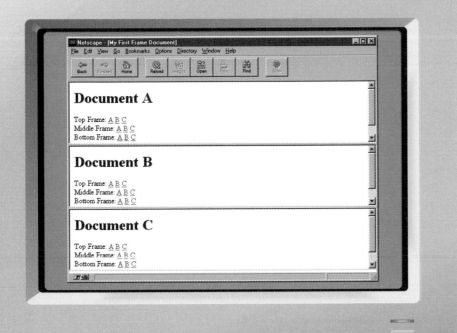

```
<HTML>
<HEAD>
<TITLE>Document A</TITLE>
</HEAD>
|
```

3 Type <HEAD> and press Enter. Then type <TITLE>**Document A**</TITLE> and press Enter. Finally, type </HEAD> and press Enter again.

```
</HEAD>
<BODY>
<H1>Document A</H1>
|
```

4 Type <BODY> and press Enter. Then type <H1>**Document A**</H1> and press Enter.

```
<BODY>
<H1>Document A</H1>
<P>Top Frame:
|
```

5 Type <P> to start your first paragraph. Then type **Top Frame:** and press Enter.

```
<P>Top Frame:
<A HREF="a.html" TARGET="frame1">A</A>
|
```

6 Here's where we'll start placing hyperlinks with target attributes. These three hyperlinks will allow the user to display different documents in the top frame. Type <A HREF="a.html" TARGET="frame1">A</A>. This link will load a.html (the document you're creating right now) into the frame named *frame1*. In the frame document you created in the last section, frame1 was the top frame.

```
<P>Top Frame:
<A HREF="a.html" TARGET="frame1">A</A>
<A HREF="b.html" TARGET="frame1">B</A>
<A HREF="c.html" TARGET="frame1">C</A>
|
```

7 Press Enter, then type <A HREF="b.html" TARGET="frame1">B</A>. This link will load a document named b.html into the top frame. Press Enter again and then type <A HREF="c.html" TARGET="frame1">C</A>. As you've probably guessed by now, this hyperlink will load c.html into the top frame. Press Enter again.

Continue to next page ▶

How to Use Targets in Frames (Continued)

```
<BR>
Bottom Frame:
<A HREF="a.html" TARGET="frame3">A</A>
<A HREF="b.html" TARGET="frame3">B</A>
<A HREF="c.html" TARGET="frame3">C</A>
</P>
|
```

▶ **10** When you're finished, type <BR> to force another line break and press Enter. Then type **Bottom Frame:** and press Enter again. Type in the hyperlinks again, with the target set to *frame3*. When you're finished, press Enter and type </P> to close the paragraph. Then press Enter again.

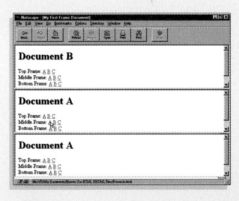

17 Now try clicking on the different hyperlinks and see what happens. You can load A, B, and C into any of the three frames. You can even fill all three frames with the same document.

TIP SHEET

▶ **For more information on hyperlinks, refer back to Chapter 6.**

▶ **You can use _SELF in place of the actual target name if the hyperlink updates the current frame. If most of your links update the current frame, using _SELF can be easier than having to specify the exact frame name each time.**

11 Type </BODY> and then press Enter. Then type </HTML>.

```
</P>
</BODY>
</HTML>
```

12 Save this document as **a.html**. Make sure that you save it in the same folder as myframe.html, which you created in the last section.

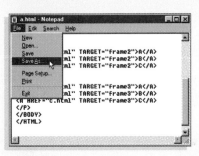

13 Repeat this process two more times, and save the files as b.html and c.html. To save a lot of typing, you can simply change the <TITLE> and <H1> tags at the top of the document and save the existing file under a new name. Just choose Save As from the File menu and type in the new file name.

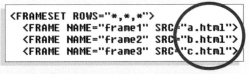

```
<FRAMESET ROWS="*,*,*">
  <FRAME NAME="frame1" SRC="a.html">
  <FRAME NAME="frame2" SRC="b.html">
  <FRAME NAME="frame3" SRC="c.html">
```

14 Open myframe.html in Notepad. Place the cursor inside the SRC attribute of the first <FRAME> tag, and change the URL from blank.html to **a.html**. Change the URLs for the next two <FRAME> tags to **b.html** and **c.html**, respectively.

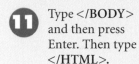

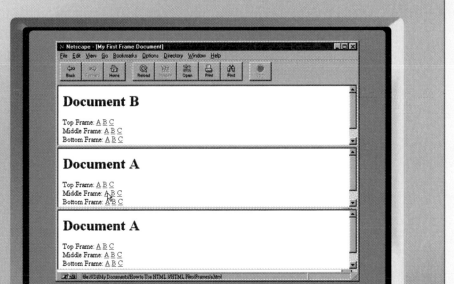

16 Launch Netscape and open myframe.html. Three frames will appear. Each of your three HTML documents, A, B, and C, will appear in a different frame.

15 Choose Save from the File menu to save the changes to myframe.html.

Extending Your Frames

In the beginning of this chapter, you learned how to create a very simple frame document. Now we'll take a look at the attributes you can include inside the <FRAMESET> and <FRAME> tags to gain finer control over the layout and appearance of your frames.

▶ **1** Open your frame document, myframe.html, in Notepad.

▶ **Avoid setting frames with absolute sizes. You have no control over the overall size of the user's Web browser, and your specified absolute sizes may be adjusted to values you did not anticipate. Use relative and percentage sizes whenever possible. If you must use an absolute size for one of your frames, be sure to use relative sizes for the others.**

▶ **If you want to create text that can be viewed by browsers that do not support frames, place a <NOFRAMES> and </NOFRAMES> tag pair between the <FRAMESET> and </FRAMESET> tag pair. Any HTML code that you place between the <NOFRAMES> tags will be ignored by frames-capable browsers. This will allow you to place a warning as well as a link to a version of your HTML document that does not require frames-capable browsers.**

```
<FRAME NAME="frame1" SRC="blank.html" scrolling="no"
NORESIZE MARGINHEIGHT=5 MARGINWIDTH=5>
```

8 You can specify desired margins for your frames using the MARGINHEIGHT and MARGINWIDTH attributes inside each <FRAME> tag. You supply the number of pixels between the frame border and the objects inside the frame. For example, to place a buffer of five pixels in all four margins, type **MARGINHEIGHT=5 MARGINWIDTH=5** inside the <FRAME> tag.

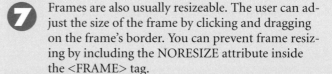

```
<FRAME NAME="frame1" SRC="blank.html" scrolling="no"
NORESIZE>
```

7 Frames are also usually resizeable. The user can adjust the size of the frame by clicking and dragging on the frame's border. You can prevent frame resizing by including the NORESIZE attribute inside the <FRAME> tag.

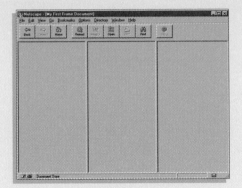

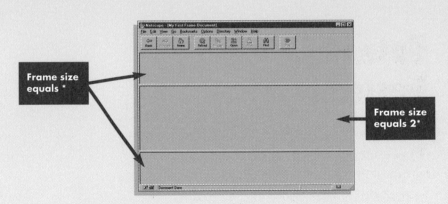

Frame size equals *

Frame size equals 2*

2 The current <FRAMESET> tag specifies that three horizontal frames, also known as Rows, of equal relative size should be created. You can change the horizontal frames to vertical ones by replacing ROWS with COLS.

3 The asterisks indicate relative sizes for each frame. Currently, each frame has a relative size of 1. You can change the relative size of any frame by placing a number in front of the asterisk for that row. For example, replace ROWS="*,*,*" with **ROWS="*,2,*"** to make the middle frame twice as big as the other two frames.

4 You can specify an absolute size for each frame by replacing the asterisk with a number. This number specifies the size of the frame in pixels. The browser will attempt to size the row to your specification, but it may adjust the size in order to fit all of the frames into the browser window. To specify an absolute size for the middle frame, type **ROWS="*,25,*"**.

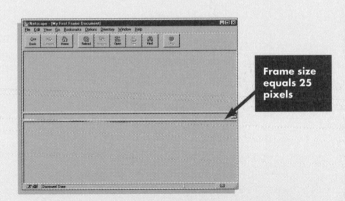

Frame size equals 25 pixels

```
<FRAME NAME="frame1" SRC="blank.html" scrolling="no">
```

6 Frames automatically appear with scroll bars inside when necessary, so that users can scroll through the contents of each frame. If you want a frame to be nonscrolling, type **SCROLLING="no"** inside the individual <FRAME> tag. If scroll bars are disabled, the user may not be able to read all of the contents in the frame.

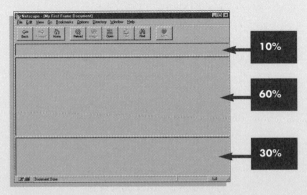

10%

60%

30%

5 You can also specify the frame size as a percentage of the overall window size. For example, you can set the three frames using percentages by typing **ROWS="10%,60%,30%"**.

How to Create Nested Frames

You have already learned how to create frame documents, fill them with HTML content, and target them with hyperlinks. However, there is still one cool frame trick that we haven't covered yet—nesting frames. It is possible to nest <FRAMESET> tag pairs to create frames within frames. In this section, you'll learn how it's done.

1 Open a new document in Notepad, and type in the lines as shown.

8 If you open newframe.html in Netscape, you'll notice that it looks a lot like the first frame document you created, but with one major difference: The bottom two frames are now aligned side by side instead of one on top of the other.

7 Save your document as newframe.html, and place it in the same folder as a.html, b.html, and c.html, which you created earlier in this chapter.

```
</HEAD>
<FRAMESET ROWS="*,*">
|
```

2 Type <FRAMESET ROWS="*,*"> to divide the screen into two frames. Then press Enter.

```
<FRAMESET ROWS="*,*">
  <FRAME SRC="a.html" NAME=frame1>
  |
```

3 Type <FRAME SRC="a.html" NAME=frame1>. This will place the document a.html in the top frame. Now press Enter again.

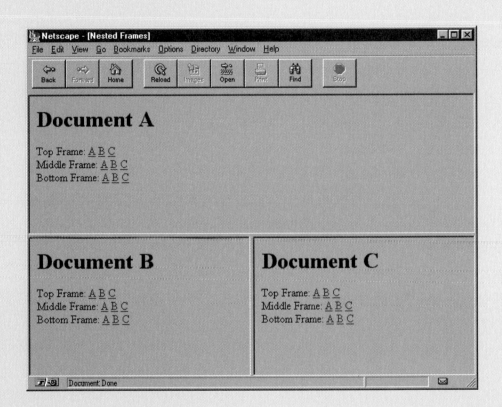

```
<FRAMESET ROWS="*,*">
  <FRAME SRC="a.html" NAME=frame1>
  <FRAMESET COLS="*,*">
  |
```

4 Instead of inserting another <FRAME> tag, we'll nest another <FRAMESET> tag pair, using COLS instead of ROWS. This will have the effect of splitting the bottom frame into two separate frames. Type <FRAMESET COLS="*,*"> and press Enter.

```
<FRAMESET COLS="*,*">
  <FRAME SRC="b.html" NAME=frame2>
  <FRAME SRC="c.html" NAME=frame3>
  |
```

5 Now, we'll create the frame declarations for the two nested frames. Type <FRAME SRC="b.html" NAME=frame2>. Then press Enter and type <FRAME SRC="c.html" NAME=frame3>. Then press Enter again.

```
    <FRAME SRC="c.html" NAME=frame3>
  </FRAMESET>
</FRAMESET>
</HTML>|
```

6 Close the nested <FRAMESET> tag by typing </FRAMESET>, and then press Enter. Then close the first <FRAMESET> tag by typing <FRAMESET> again and pressing Enter. When you're finished, type </HTML>.

CHAPTER 15

Using the Internet Explorer Extensions

 Netscape is the most popular of all Web browsers, but it's not the only one out there. One browser that HTML authors need to be particularly aware of is Microsoft's Internet Explorer.

Internet Explorer was introduced with Windows 95, and it comes packaged with the Windows 95 Plus! pack. It is also available for free from Microsoft's Web site at http://www.microsoft.com. Internet Explorer is tightly integrated with Windows 95, and it is the Web browser of choice for many Windows 95 users. For that reason alone, HTML authors need to be familiar with Internet Explorer's capabilities and limitations.

In this chapter, you'll learn about Internet Explorer's extensions to HTML. In addition to its support for many of the Netscape extensions, Internet Explorer adds many new tricks for HTML authors to use in their documents. Among these are support for audio and video, colors for tables, and typeface and color control for fonts.

How to Use Internet Explorer's Formatting Extensions

O ne of the most versatile extensions to HTML is Internet Explorer's ability to display exact typefaces. Whereas most browsers are limited to the default typeface (usually Times New Roman), Internet Explorer can display HTML text in any typeface you specify. The only requirement is that the typeface must be installed on the reader's system.

Internet Explorer also adds a number of additional formatting extensions, including the ability to specify font colors and to include watermarked, or nonscrolling, background images.

1 Open a new document in Notepad and type in the lines as shown above.

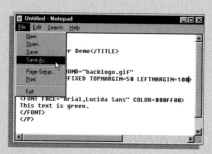

9 Save your file in Notepad as explore.html, and leave it open for the exercise in the next section.

```
<BODY BACKGROUND="backlogo.gif"
BGPROPERTIES=FIXED TOPMARGIN=50 LEFTMARGIN=100>
```

8 To change the left margin, place the cursor inside the <BODY> tag and type LEFTMARGIN=, followed by a number. This represents the number of pixels in the margin. To specify a top margin, type TOPMARGIN=, followed by a pixel value. For example, to set the top margin to 50 pixels and the left margin to 100 pixels, type TOPMARGIN=50 LEFTMARGIN=100.

7 Internet Explorer allows you to set a left and top margin for the document. Any HTML elements, except background images, will be displayed within the confines of the margins you specify. The margins are measured in pixels, and the default for both is 0.

TIP SHEET

▶ When you specify a particular font name, it will only display correctly if the end user has the exact same font installed. For that reason, try to stick with the basic fonts that are included with Windows.

▶ For more information on background images, refer back to Chapter 9, "Advanced Graphics Techniques."

```
<BODY>

<P>
<FONT FACE="">|
</P>

</BODY>
</HTML>
```

2 Internet Explorer allows you to specify an exact typeface for text using the <FONT> tag and the FACE attribute. Type <**FONT FACE=""**> wherever you'd like the new formatting to begin in your document.

```
<P>
<FONT FACE="Arial,Lucida Sans|">
</P>
```

3 Now you need to specify a list of font names, in order of preference, inside the quotation marks. Internet Explorer will use the first font in your list that is also installed on the user's system. For example, to set the typeface to Arial with a second choice of Lucida Sans, type **Arial,Lucida Sans**. If none of the fonts in your list is installed on the user's system, Internet Explorer will display the text in the user's default font.

```
<P>
<FONT FACE="Arial,Lucida Sans" COLOR=#008000>
This text is green.
</FONT>
</P>
```

4 Internet Explorer can also display any selection of text in a different color using the COLOR attribute inside the <FONT> tag. The COLOR attribute is specified with an RGB hexadecimal code, preceded by a pound sign. For example, to display text in green, type **COLOR=#008000** inside the <FONT> tag. Then type **This text is green** after the <FONT> tag. Finally, type </**FONT**> to mark the end of the font effects.

Left margin   Colored font

Watermark background

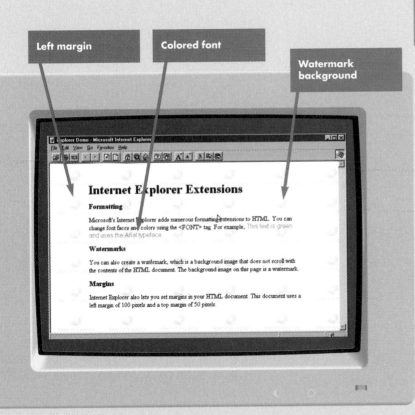

Internet Explorer Extensions

Formatting

Microsoft's Internet Explorer adds numerous formatting extensions to HTML. You can change font faces and colors using the <FONT> tag. For example, This text is green and uses the Arial typeface.

Watermarks

You can also create a watermark, which is a background image that does not scroll with the contents of the HTML document. The background image on this page is a watermark.

Margins

Internet Explorer also lets you set margins in your HTML document. This document uses a left margin of 100 pixels and a top margin of 50 pixels.

```
<BODY BACKGROUND="backlogo.gif">|
```

5 You can create a watermark image in your HTML document using the <BODY> tag. A watermark is just like a background image, except that it does not scroll with the rest of the document. To create a watermark, type **BACKGROUND=** inside the <BODY> tag, followed by the URL of the image in quotation marks. For example, to include the image backlogo.gif as your background image, type **BACKGROUND="backlogo.gif"**.

```
<BODY BACKGROUND="backlogo.gif"
BGPROPERTIES=FIXED>|
```

6 Next, add the attribute **BGPROPERTIES=FIXED** inside the <BODY> tag. Now, when the user reads your document, the background image is fixed in place and will not scroll.

How to Play Sound and Video Clips with Internet Explorer

Internet Explorer provides numerous extensions to the <IMG> tag in HTML. Most notably, it supports the playing of AVI format videos inside your HTML document. AVI is short for *audio video interleave*, a common format for video on the Microsoft Windows operating system.

Internet Explorer accomplishes this with the dynamic source attribute (DYNSRC), which is placed inside the <IMG> tag. The video playback is handled directly inside the Internet Explorer browser window, so the video appears to be part of your document.

TIP SHEET

▶ Internet Explorer only supports AVI format videos. If you have a video in another format, such as QuickTime, Internet Explorer will not display it.

▶ You can use both FILEOPEN and MOUSEOVER together with the START attribute. Typing START=MOUSEOVER,FILEOPEN will cause the video to be played once when the HTML document is loaded, and once every time the mouse cursor passes over the video clip.

▶ Keep your sound and video files as compact as possible. Internet Explorer will need to load the entire sound or video file in order to display it. This could take a very long time, especially with a slow Internet connection.

1 To insert an AVI video into your HTML document, use the <IMG> tag with the DYNSRC attribute. For example, to insert an AVI video named movie.avi, type **<IMG DYNSRC="movie.avi">** anywhere inside the body section of your HTML document.

8 You can repeat the sound with the LOOP attribute, which works the same way with sounds as it does with video clips. For example, to play the boom.wav sound three times when the document is loaded, type **LOOP=3** inside the <BGSOUND> tag.

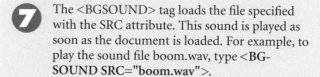

7 The <BGSOUND> tag loads the file specified with the SRC attribute. This sound is played as soon as the document is loaded. For example, to play the sound file boom.wav, type <BGSOUND SRC="boom.wav">.

```
<IMG DYNSRC="movie.avi" SRC="movie.gif">
```

2 You should also specify a still image, preferably a frame from the video, using the SRC attribute. This still image will be displayed in other browsers instead of the video. Add **SRC=** to the image tag, followed by the URL of the still image in quotes.

```
<IMG DYNSRC="movie.avi" SRC="movie.gif"
LOOP=INFINITE>
```

3 Placing the LOOP attribute inside the IMG tag allows you to specify how many times the video clip should play. You can instruct the browser to play the video a specific number of times, or to loop infinitely. For example, to play the video for five complete cycles, type **LOOP=5** inside the <IMG> tag. To play the video infinitely, type **LOOP=INFINITE**.

Inline AVI video

Video playback controls

```
<IMG DYNSRC="movie.avi" SRC="movie.gif"
LOOP=INFINITE START=MOUSEOVER>
```

4 You can also specify when the video should start playing by using the START attribute inside the <IMG> tag. The video can start either once the HTML document is loaded, or when the user places the mouse cursor over the video. To start the video as soon as the HTML document is open, type **START=FILEOPEN**. To wait until the user places the cursor over the video image, type **START=MOUSEOVER**.

```
<IMG DYNSRC="movie.avi" SRC="movie.gif"
LOOP=INFINITE START=MOUSEOVER CONTROLS>
```

6 You can add sound to your document with the <BGSOUND> tag, which can be placed anywhere inside the body section. You can use digitized sound samples in .WAV or .AU format as well as MIDI music files.

5 You can place a set of video playback controls underneath your video clip by typing **CONTROLS** inside the <IMG> tag. The controls allow the user to pause, fast forward, rewind, and play the video clip.

How to Use Scrolling Text Marquees

Sometimes you want to get a simple message across to your readers and you want it to stand out from the rest of the document. Internet Explorer lets you create flashy text messages with scrolling marquees.

Marquees work as electronic billboards. The text is animated and it scrolls across the marquee, where it easily catches the eye. You can control the speed, style, and direction of the text.

```
<MARQUEE>Sale! 50% Off</MARQUEE>|
```

▶ **1** To place a scrolling text marquee in your HTML document, type <MARQUEE>, followed by the text and a closing </MARQUEE> tag. This will cause the text inside the tag to scroll across the screen. For example, to scroll the words *Sale! 50% Off!*, type **<MARQUEE>Sale! 50% Off</MARQUEE>**.

```
<MARQUEE BEHAVIOR=SLIDE DIRECTION=RIGHT
HEIGHT=40 WIDTH=50% LOOP=5 SCROLLAMOUNT
SCROLLDELAY=100 BGCOLOR=#008800>
```

8 If you want to change the background color of the marquee, use the BGCOLOR attribute inside the <MARQUEE> tag. The color must be specified using an RGB hexadecimal code and preceded with a pound sign. For example, to set the background color of the marquee to light green, type **BGCOLOR=#008800**.

```
<MARQUEE BEHAVIOR=SLIDE DIRECTION=RIGHT
HEIGHT=40 WIDTH=50% LOOP=5 SCROLLAMOUNT=1
SCROLLDELAY=100>
```

7 You can also control the speed of the marquee text display using the SCROLLDELAY attribute. This attribute specifies the number of milliseconds that will elapse between each redraw of the marquee text. For example, to set the delay to 100 milliseconds, type **SCROLLDELAY=100** inside the <MARQUEE> tag.

`<MARQUEE BEHAVIOR=SLIDE>`

2 There are several attributes that you can add to the <MARQUEE> tag that will allow you to control its appearance. First, you can control the style of the marquee using the BEHAVIOR tag. You can make the text scroll, slide, or alternate (bounce back and forth) inside the marquee. The default style is scrolling text. To change this to sliding text, type **BEHAVIOR=SLIDE** inside the <MARQUEE> tag.

`<MARQUEE BEHAVIOR=SLIDE DIRECTION=RIGHT>`

3 By default, text in a <MARQUEE> tag moves from the right side of the marquee to the left. You can reverse the direction by typing **DIRECTION=RIGHT** inside the <MARQUEE> tag.

`<MARQUEE BEHAVIOR=SLIDE DIRECTION=RIGHT HEIGHT=40 WIDTH=50%>`

4 You can specify the height and width of the marquee by placing HEIGHT and WIDTH attributes inside the <MARQUEE> tag. The height and width can be expressed as either specific pixel values or a percentage of the screen. For example, to set the marquee to be exactly 40 pixels high with a width of 50 percent of the visible screen, you would type **HEIGHT=40 WIDTH=50%** inside the <MARQUEE> tag.

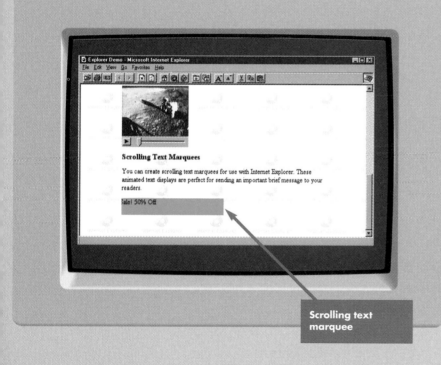

Scrolling text marquee

`<MARQUEE BEHAVIOR=SLIDE DIRECTION=RIGHT HEIGHT=40 WIDTH=50% LOOP=5>`

5 You can specify how many times the marquee text will loop by using the LOOP attribute inside the <MARQUEE> tag. For example, to set the marquee text to loop five times, type **LOOP=5**. If you do not use the LOOP attribute, the marquee text will cycle infinitely.

`<MARQUEE BEHAVIOR=SLIDE DIRECTION=RIGHT HEIGHT=40 WIDTH=50% LOOP=5 SCROLLAMOUNT=1>`

6 The SCROLLAMOUNT attribute allows you to specify how many pixels the marquee moves each time it is redrawn. This directly affects the smoothness of the scrolling text as well as the speed with which it moves across the screen. For example, to get the text to scroll slowly and smoothly across the screen one pixel at a time, type **SCROLLAMOUNT=1** inside the <MARQUEE> tag.

Extending Tables with Internet Explorer

Internet Explorer supports a handful of extensions to change colors of HTML tables. Normally, HTML tables appear in the same color as the background and use white and dark gray borders for a 3-D effect. With Internet Explorer, you can assign a different background color as well as different border colors for your tables. You can even assign a different background color for each individual cell.

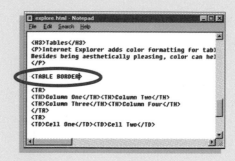

▶ **1** Open the HTML document that contains your table and place the cursor inside the opening <TABLE> tag of the table you want to modify.

7 Save your modified HTML document, and then view the new table with Internet Explorer.

`<TABLE BORDER BGCOLOR=#00ff00>`

2 You can change the background color for the entire table by using the BG-COLOR attribute inside the <TABLE> tag. The BGCOLOR attribute uses an RGB hexadecimal code, preceded by a pound sign. For example, to set the background color of the table to green, type **BGCOLOR=#00ff00**.

`<TD BGCOLOR=#0000ff>Cell Three</TD>`

3 You can also place a BGCOLOR attribute inside a <TR>, <TH>, or <TD> tag, even if you have already specified a background color for the entire table. Background color settings for individual elements, such as cells or rows, take precedence over settings for the entire table. To change the background color for a single cell to blue, type **BGCOLOR=#0000ff** inside that cell's <TD> tag.

`<TABLE BORDER BGCOLOR=#00ff00 BORDERCOLOR=#8080ff>`

4 You can also change the color of the table border by placing the BORDERCOLOR attribute inside the <TABLE> tag. The BORDERCOLOR attribute also uses an RGB hexadecimal code. To set the color of the border to a light shade of blue, type **BORDERCOLOR=#8080ff** inside the <TABLE> tag.

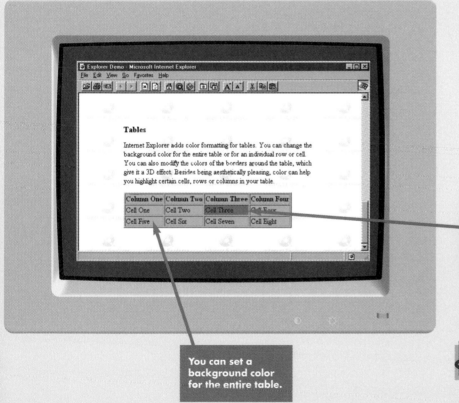

You can change the background color of individual cells.

You can set a background color for the entire table.

`<TABLE BORDER BGCOLOR=#00ff00 BORDERCOLOR=#8080ff`
`BORDERCOLORLIGHT=#e0e0ff>`

5 You can also change the color of the table's outer borders, which give a table its 3-D effect. To change the color of the upper and left borders (the light colored ones), use an RGB code with the BORDERCOLORLIGHT attribute. For example, to set these two borders to a very faint shade of blue, type **BORDERCOLORLIGHT=#e0e0ff** inside the <TABLE> tag.

`<TABLE BORDER BGCOLOR=#00ff00 BORDERCOLOR=#8080ff`
`BORDERCOLORLIGHT=#e0e0ff BORDERCOLORDARK=#000080>`

6 To set the color for the other two borders, use the BOR-DERCOLORDARK attribute. For example, to set the color for these two borders to a deep shade of blue, type **BOR-DERCOLORDARK=#000080** inside the <TABLE> tag.

TRY IT!

Lawn Birds, Inc. wants to update their online catalog to take advantage of the Internet Explorer extensions. However, they want you to design the HTML document in such a way that any user will be able to view it, even if they're not using Internet Explorer as their browser.

This is an opportunity to practice the techniques you learned in the previous chapter, as well as to build an understanding of how the Internet Explorer extensions can be incorporated into documents without making them incompatible with other Web browsers.

1

Start Notepad and open catalog.html, which you created in the third Try It!

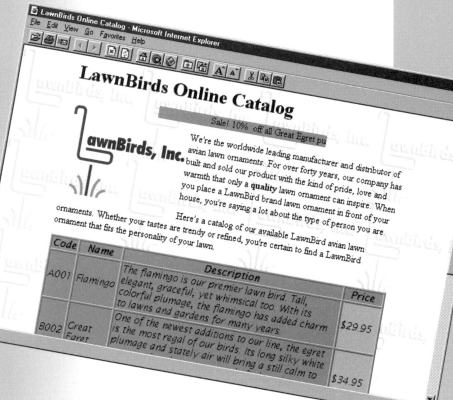

Turn Word Wrap on.

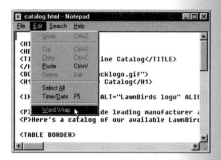

Locate the <BODY> tag. This document already has a background image of the LawnBirds, Inc. logo. Place the cursor after the URL of the logo.

```
<BODY BACKGROUND="backlogo.gif">
<H1>LawnBirds Online Catalog</H1>
```

Currently, the background logo scrolls with the text of the page. To freeze the background in place as though it were a watermark, type **BGPROPERTIES=FIXED**. When viewed with Internet Explorer, the logo will not scroll. It will still scroll as usual when viewed with other Web browsers.

```
<BODY BACKGROUND="backlogo.gif"
BGPROPERTIES=FIXED>
```

Now, add a left margin of 100 pixels to the <BODY> tag by typing **LEFTMARGIN=100**. Adding margins to HTML documents is purely stylistic, but it can make some types of documents easier to read.

```
<BODY BACKGROUND="backlogo.gif"
BGPROPERTIES=FIXED LEFTMARGIN=100>
```

LawnBirds, Inc. wants you to incorporate their company theme song, "It's a LawnBirds World," into their online catalog. They have provided a MIDI version for you to include, named lawn-wrld.mid. Because you don't really have this file on your system, you can use another MIDI or WAV sound file in its place.

Place the cursor after the <BODY> tag and press Enter. Then type **<BGSOUND="lawnwrld.mid" LOOP=INFINITE>**. If you used a different file as the background sound, type that file name in place of lawnwrld.mid.

```
<BODY BACKGROUND="backlogo.gif"
BGPROPERTIES=FIXED LEFTMARGIN=100>
<BGSOUND="lawnwrld.mid" LOOP=INFINITE>
```

Now you can begin enhancing the table, which displays all the different products in the LawnBirds line. First of all, you can change the font displayed in the table.

Insert a blank line after the <TABLE> tag and type **<FONT FACE="Lucida Sans,Arial">**. Internet Explorer will attempt to display the table text in Lucida Sans. If that font is not installed on the user's system, it will try to display it in Arial. If neither font is available, the text will be displayed in the default font.

```
<TABLE BORDER>
<FONT FACE="Lucida Sans,Arial">
```

Continue to next page ▶

TRY IT!

Continue
below

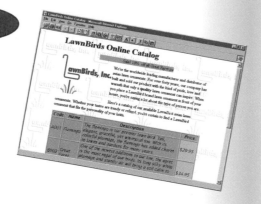

10

```
<TABLE BORDER BGCOLOR=#ef9cb5>
```

Now change the background color of
the table to "LawnBirds Pink," which
has an RGB hexadecimal code of
#ef9cb5. Place the cursor inside the
<TABLE> tag, after the word *BORDER*
and type **BGCOLOR=#ef9cb5**.

11

```
<TABLE BORDER BGCOLOR=#ef9cb5
BORDERCOLORLIGHT=#fbe3eb>
```

Now change the colors of the light and
dark edges of the borders, which give
the table its 3-D effect. Type **BORDER-
COLORLIGHT=#fbe3eb** inside the
<TABLE> tag to change the light col-
ored borders from white to a light pink.

12

```
<TABLE BORDER BGCOLOR=#ef9cb5
BORDERCOLORLIGHT=#fbe3eb BORDERCOLORDARK=#e04372>
```

Type **BORDERCOLORDARK=#e04372** to
change the dark colored borders from dark
gray to a dark shade of pink. The table color-
ing effects are purely cosmetic, but will make
your table look much better when viewed by
Internet Explorer. These changes will not affect the table when viewed by other browsers.

13

```
charm to lawns and gardens for many
years.</TD><TD>$29.95</TD>
```

LawnBirds, Inc. wants the table's price column
to be highlighted. You can do this by changing
the background color for each cell in the column. Place the cursor inside the first price
cell's <TD> tag.

14

```
years.</TD><TD BGCOLOR=#e4c2d1>$29.95</TD>
```

Type **BGCOLOR=#e4c2d1** inside the
<TD> tag. This will change the back-
ground color to a lighter shade of pink.

15

Repeat the previous step for each of the remaining cells that contain price information.

16

```
<H1>LawnBirds Online Catalog</H1>

<IMG SRC="logo.gif" ALT="LawnBirds logo"
ALIGN=LEFT HEIGHT=153 WIDTH=203>
```

LawnBirds,
Inc. wants to place a scrolling text
marquee at the top of this document
to convey last-minute updates and
sale information. Place the cursor on
a new line immediately before the
document's <H1> headline tag.

```
<H1>LawnBirds Online Catalog</H1>
<MARQUEE>Sale! 10% off all Great Egret
purchases this summer. Call 1-800-555-LAWN
to place your order today.</MARQUEE>
```

Type <MARQUEE>Sale! 10% off all Great Egret purchases this summer. Call 1-800-555-LAWN to place your order today.</MARQUEE>.

```
<MARQUEE BGCOLOR=#ef9cb5>Sale! 10% off all
```

Now place the cursor inside the opening <MARQUEE> tag and type **BGCOLOR=#ef9cb5**. This will set the background color of the marquee text to "LawnBirds Pink," the same color as the table you just enhanced.

```
<MARQUEE BGCOLOR=#ef9cb5 WIDTH=50%>Sale! 10%
```

Set the marquee width to 50% of the screen by typing **WIDTH=50%** inside the <MARQUEE> tag.

```
<CENTER>
<MARQUEE BGCOLOR=#ef9cb5 WIDTH=50%>Sale! 10%
off all Great Egret purchases this summer.
Call 1-800-555-LAWN to place your order
today.</MARQUEE>
</CENTER>
```

Internet Explorer also recognizes the Netscape <CENTER> tag. Type in the opening <**CENTER**> and closing </**CENTER**> tags around the <MARQUEE> tag pair. This will center the scrolling text marquee on the screen.

Choose Save from the File menu to save your changes.

Launch Internet Explorer and choose Open from the File menu.

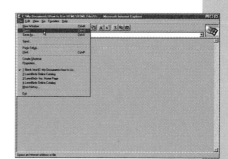

Click on the Open File button and then locate catalog.html.

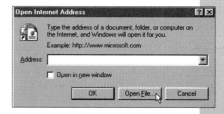

Click on the Open button to load the enhanced LawnBirds, Inc. catalog

with Internet Explorer. Note the changes you made, including the colored table and the scrolling text marquee. You should also open catalog.html with other browsers, such as Netscape, for comparison.

CHAPTER 16

Converting Existing Documents to HTML

 So far, you've learned just about everything you need to know to create HTML documents from scratch. But what about converting existing documents to HTML? The prospect of having to retype documents and insert the appropriate HTML codes by hand isn't very promising, even for the most experienced HTML wizards.

Fortunately, there are plenty of tools available to convert existing documents to HTML quickly. If you're lucky enough to have your documents in Microsoft Word format, conversion is a snap. However, even if your documents are in plain text, the dirty work of inserting paragraph markers, line breaks, and heading tags can be done automatically by the right tools.

How to Convert Text Files to HTML with HotDog Professional

If you have a lot of plain text files that you need to quickly convert to HTML, one of the best tools available is HotDog Professional. One of the many features of this popular HTML editor is its ability to quickly convert existing text documents to HTML after you select just a few simple options. HotDog Professional automates most of the task, and produces a valid HTML document in mere seconds.

HotDog Professional is available as shareware, and you can evaluate it for free for 30 days. It is well worth a look. You can download a copy from Sausage Software's Web site at http://www.sausage.com.

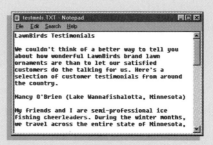

1 Locate the text file you want to convert to HTML.

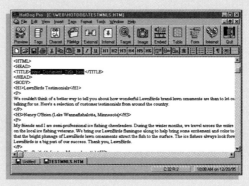

11 Open your new HTML files with either HotDog Professional or Notepad and make any necessary manual changes, such as inserting a title for the document. Save your changes when you are finished.

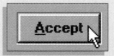

10 Click on the Accept button to convert your text files to HTML. The conversion happens almost instantly, and HotDog Professional saves the converted files with file names similar to your original text files, except with an .htm extension. By default, HotDog Professional will save the new files in the program's main folder.

TIP SHEET

▸ The conversion process works best with text files that are simple and follow a regular pattern, such as a heading followed by a paragraph. If your text file has several different sections, you may want to break it up into smaller text files first.

▸ HotDog Professional is a full-featured HTML editor, and you may decide to start using it instead of Notepad for all of your HTML document writing. The best part about HotDog Professional is that it's shareware, which means you can try it before you decide whether to purchase it.

3 In the Text to HTML Converter dialog box, select the appropriate options. You'll almost always want to select the first option, Change one or more blank lines to <P>. Blank lines in text files usually indicate separate paragraphs.

2 Launch HotDog Professional and choose Convert to HTML from the Tools menu.

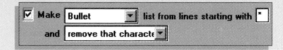

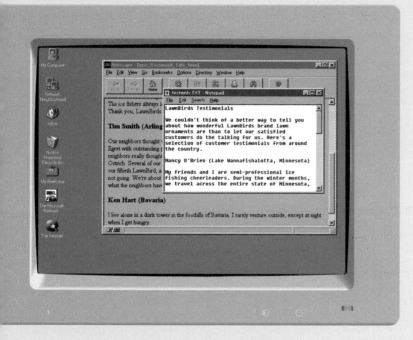

4 The second option concerns the creation of lists. If your text file contains bulleted lists, you can automatically convert them to HTML lists. Choose the type of list you'd like to create, along with the character used in the text file to denote a list item.

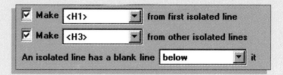

5 The second group of options deals with creating headings. If your text file uses single lines of text to separate sections, you can convert them to HTML headings. Select the type of HTML heading you'd like to create. You can choose a separate heading style for the very first line in your text file.

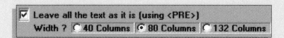

6 You can also leave the entire text file as it is by choosing to convert it to preformatted text. This option also allows you to choose the column width for the resulting HTML file.

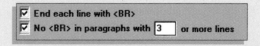

7 You have the option of inserting a line break after each line. This is a good idea if your text file contains a number of short lines that should not be converted into paragraphs.

9 Select the files you'd like to convert. You can choose multiple files by pressing the Ctrl key as you select each one. You can also use wildcard characters to select multiple files. When you're finished, click on the OK button.

8 When you're done setting the conversion options, click on the Convert Files button.

How to Convert Microsoft Word Documents to HTML

Microsoft provides an add-on for Word called Internet Assistant. This powerful set of tools is the perfect vehicle for anyone familiar with Word who also wants to publish HTML documents. Internet Assistant handles all of the HTML coding, allowing you to spend your effort on the documents themselves, and not the coding necessary to make them visible on the Web.

Internet Assistant is available for free, and requires Word 6.0 or later. You can download it from Microsoft's Web site at http://www.microsoft.com/msoffice/freestuf/msword/download/ia/default.htm.

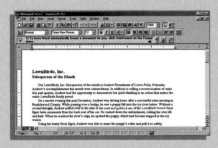

1 Open the Microsoft Word document you want to convert to HTML.

TIP SHEET

▶ **Internet Assistant is a full-featured HTML editor, although it does not support all of the HTML3 standards. However, it's a free add-on for Word users, and you may decide to use it as your regular HTML editor.**

▶ **Internet Assistant's built-in Web browser is crude but effective. If you have a working Internet connection, you can browse the Web from inside Word. Just switch to Web Browse view, and you'll be able to test out all the links you have placed in your HTML document.**

▶ **WordPerfect users can also add a plug-in to their word processor that will help convert documents to HTML. The plug-in, known as Internet Publisher, requires WordPerfect 6.1 or later. It is available for download at the WordPerfect FTP site at ftp://ftp.wordperfect.com/pub/wpapps/intpub/wpipzip.exe.**

8 When you're finished editing your document, save it once more as an HTML file.

7 If you switch back to HTML Edit mode from the View menu, you can insert additional HTML codes and markup by selecting these options from the Insert menu.

2 Choose Save As from the File menu.

3 Change the file type in the Save as type list box to HTML. Word will automatically change the file extension to .htm. Click on the Save button to save the file.

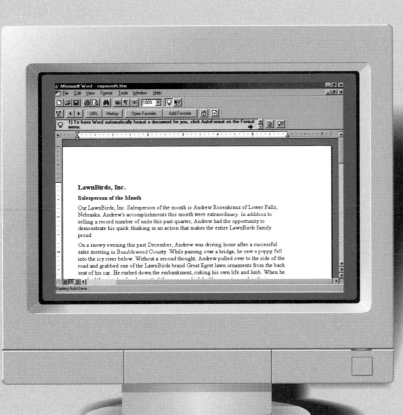

4 Word will automatically convert your document to HTML, adding all of the necessary tags. This process takes only a few seconds, and when it's finished, you'll have a complete HTML document.

5 You can see the actual HTML source code by selecting HTML Source from the View menu.

6 You can preview the HTML document by choosing Web Browse from the View menu. This will launch Internet Assistant's built-in Web browsing software.

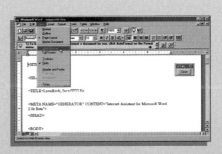

CHAPTER 17

Working with Multiple HTML Documents

 One of the most difficult tasks you'll encounter as an HTML author will be organizing all of your documents together to build a comprehensive and coherent Web site. Top-notch Web sites are more than just collections of HTML documents—the best sites are pulled together with consistent and thoughtful design.

In this chapter, you'll learn a few simple guidelines for pulling together your documents in order to build a Web site that is easy to navigate and understand. With a little effort, you can easily create and maintain the type of high-quality and compelling Web site that users will come back to again and again.

How to Organize Multiple HTML Documents

One of the first tasks you'll need to tackle when deciding how to put together multiple Web pages is how you'll physically store your documents on the server. You may be tempted to throw everything—all of your HTML documents, images, sounds, and other files—into a single directory on the server. This chaotic style of organization will appear easier in the beginning, but will eventually wreak havoc on your ability to maintain and update the Web site on an ongoing basis.

This section will give you a few tips, tricks, and pointers to get you started on organizing an efficient and easily maintainable Web site.

1 Plan out your Web site on paper before you begin writing any HTML code. A rough sketch of all the documents you will need to prepare can help put your entire site in perspective and help you organize and create your Web site effectively. Planning an interactive multimedia Web site with plain pencil and paper may seem strange at first, but the important idea here is to plan ahead.

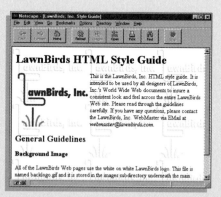

5 Write a brief style guide that explains how headings, horizontal rules, and other HTML elements should appear in your documents. This is especially helpful if more than one person will be creating HTML documents for your Web site, and it will ensure that all of your HTML documents are consistent. You might even want to create your style guide as an HTML document for easy reference and clear examples.

2 Use subdirectories to separate different sections of your site. Each subdirectory can hold all of the relevant documents for a particular section. For example, create a subdirectory called *budget* to hold all of the HTML documents related to budget issues.

3 Create a special subdirectory called *images* to store all of your GIF and JPEG images in. If you use the same image, such as a logo, in several documents, it's much easier to have all of the documents point to one image file in a common subdirectory. For example, the URL to an image stored in a common images subdirectory might look like <A HREF="images/mylogo.gif">.

4 Develop a consistent look and feel for all of the documents in your Web site. If you use particular colors and background images in your documents, repeat those colors and images in all of your documents.

How to Use Navigational Aids

Providing easy ways to navigate through your pages is another crucial aspect of building an effective Web site. As with the overall organization, consistency is the most important part of designing ways to navigate through your documents.

In this section, you'll learn a few tips and tricks for creating simple icons and menus to make navigating your Web site easier and more productive.

1 One of the most useful navigational aids is the button bar menu. This is usually a clickable image map that contains links to other parts of the Web site. If you maintain a large site with many documents, including a button bar or similar type of menu is a must.

5 Above all, be sure to maintain a consistent style and location for your navigational aids. Use the same button bars, icons, and menus throughout your Web site. If you make your Web site easy to navigate and understand, your readers will be more likely to visit again.

TIP SHEET

▶ **You don't need to create icons from scratch. There are many collections of icons available on the Web. A listing of icon collections can be found at http://www.yahoo.com/Computers_ and_Internet/Internet/World_Wide_ Web/Programming/Icons/.**

▶ **For more information on image maps, refer back to Chapters 12 and 13.**

2 If you include a clickable image map, be sure to also include an alternative text-only button bar as well. This way, users with browsers that do not support graphics will still be able to navigate around your Web site.

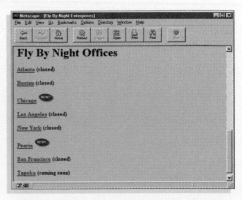

3 If your HTML documents follow a particular order, you should include icons with arrows. These images should be hyperlinks that point to the previous and next documents in the reading sequence. You should also include an icon that allows the reader to quickly return to the first or "top" document in the sequence.

4 If your documents are constantly updated, it's a good idea to include icons that show which items are new and updated. Place these icons next to the hyperlinks that point to the new or updated documents.

CHAPTER 18

The Future of HTML

 The Internet moves rapidly, and the World Wide Web is the fastest growing segment. It is evolving so quickly, in fact, that several significant changes to the Web and HTML were announced during the development of this book.

In this chapter, you'll get a sneak peek at some of the future directions of the World Wide Web. These include exciting advances such as Shockwave, the Adobe Acrobat Amber reader, and the Java programming language. You'll also learn how HTML plays a crucial role in bringing all these new technologies together on the World Wide Web.

Finally, because the Web is a constantly changing landscape, you'll learn the best places to turn for keeping updated with the newest and coolest Internet technology.

Java

J ava is a very exciting new development on the World Wide Web. It is a complete programming language, developed by Sun Microsystems and designed specifically for creating interactive applications on the Internet. Java has the potential to revolutionize the ways in which the World Wide Web is used.

Java is a simple, platform-independent, object-oriented language. That means Java *applets*—miniature applications—can be run on any machine with a Java-capable browser. In other words, the same Java application can be run on a PC, Mac, or UNIX workstation. Java is based on C++, and experienced programmers can learn it very quickly. Java also includes many security features designed to protect end-user systems and data.

Java is still in its early stages, and its full potential probably won't be realized for at least a few months. In the meantime, here are some examples of cool things that Java can do.

1 Java allows you to create both simple and complex animations. You can even create interactive animated 3-D models. For a list of 3-D Java applets, visit Gamelan, the directory and registry of Java resources at http:\\www.gamelan.com.

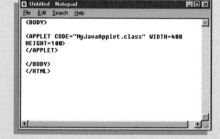

6 You can easily embed a Java applet inside your HTML document. Simply place an <**APPLET**> and </**APPPLET**> tag pair in your document. The <**APPLET**> tag requires the URL of the Java applet, which is specified using the CODE attribute.

TIP SHEET

▶ **For more information on Java, visit the Java home page at http://java.sun.com.**

▶ **There is a comprehensive collection of Java applets and resources stored on a site called Gamelan. You can visit that site at http://www.gamelan.com.**

2 With Java, you can create complex interactive graphical applications, such as this Impressionist paint program. Java's interpreted language, modeled after C++, gives programmers very powerful tools for designing Web-based interactive applications.

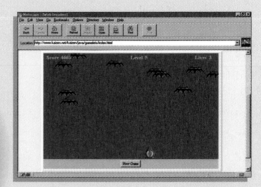

3 You can build real-time interactive games on the Web. Although Java is not well suited for graphics-intensive games, you can create a number of simple games with this language.

4 You can create a scrolling text billboard, much like a stock quote ticker. This works on the same principle as Microsoft's Internet Explorer <MARQUEE> HTML extension, but with considerably more flexibility.

5 You can use Java applets as educational tools. Fully interactive and animated tutorials can be placed on the Web using Java.

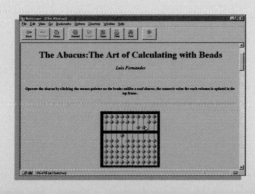

Plug-Ins

New technologies are finding their way onto the World Wide Web at an unprecedented rate. Popular Web browsers, such as Netscape Navigator and Microsoft's Internet Explorer, allow third-party *plug-ins* that enable different file formats, including interactive movies, which can be viewed from inside Web browsers, instead of downloaded and viewed with external applications.

The wide array of available plug-ins provides many new opportunities for HTML authors, but it can also cause headaches. Although most of the plug-ins are freely available, only a limited number of browsers support them. Also, there's no guarantee tht those visiting your Web page have installed the necessary plug-in modules to view the contents of your HTML documents. If you plan to use content that requires a plug-in module, be sure to explain what's needed to fully view your document and provide the necessary links to the plug-in downloads.

Here's a brief look at some of the more popular plug-ins available for Netscape.

▶ **1** VRML, which is short for *Virtual Reality Modeling Language*, is a standard scripting language for building interactive 3-D worlds on the World Wide Web. VRML worlds work like HTML pages, except that instead of relying on static links to move from page to page, users of VRML navigate through a site in real time. WebFX from Paper Software is a VRML plug-in for Netscape browsers. It is available at http://www.paperinc.com/.

5 You can incorporate video into your HTML documents with VDOLive, which compresses video images without compromising quality on the receiving end. VDOLive automatically determines the quality of the video, measured in frames per second, based on the speed of the reader's Internet connection.

TIP SHEET

▶ **Netscape maintains a list of available plug-ins for its browser at http://home.netscape.com/ comprod/products/navigator/ version_2.0/plugins/index.html.**

▶ **You can also find a list of plug-ins for several Web browsers at http://cwsapps.texas.net/ plugin.html.**

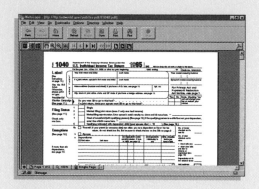

2 The Amber plug-in for Netscape allows users to read Adobe Acrobat .PDF files from inside the Netscape browser. PDF, which is short for *Portable Document Format,* is a popular cross-platform document format on the Internet. It allows authors to create a very specific layout for their documents, complete with fonts and graphics. This type of document previously required a separate external viewer, but the Amber plug-in now makes .PDF files viewable directly from Netscape. You can download the Amber plug-in from Adobe's Web site at http://www.adobe.com/Amber/Index.html.

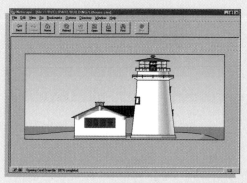

3 The Corel CMX plug-in allows the Netscape browser to view Corel CMX format vector graphics files directly in the Netscape browser window. Vector graphics files are re-sizable without image quality loss. The plug-in allows you to view CMX files separately or inside an HTML document with the <EMBED> tag. For example, to include a reference to a CMX vector file in your docu-ment, you would type <**EMBED SRC="file-name.cmx" width=100 height=100**>, replacing the height and width attributes with your desired values. Users would need to have the CMX viewer plug-in installed to see the image in your document. You can download the CMX viewer from the Corel Web site at http://www.corel.com/corelcmx/.

4 Macromedia's Shockwave plug-in is one of the most exciting add-ons available for Netscape. Shockwave allows HTML authors to incorporate Macromedia Director movies into their HTML documents. Anyone with the Shockwave plug-in can automatically view the movies, which allow for interactive feedback from the user. To download the Shockwave plug-in or learn more about in-corporating Director movies into your HTML documents, visit Macromedia's Web site at http://www.macromedia.com.

APPENDIX

HTML Quick Reference

Even the most accomplished HTML author often needs to refer back to a listing of HTML tags when putting together complex documents. Many HTML tags support several attributes, and can be used in many different ways. Keeping all the details of HTML committed to memory is close to impossible. This reference guide is designed to help you quickly recall the HTML tags and attributes you've learned about in this book.

HTML tags are divided into sections based on tag type. For each HTML tag, a description and list of possible attributes are provided. If the HTML tag is only supported by HTML3, Netscape, or Internet Explorer, that limitation is also noted. This information is taken from the HTML 3.0 draft specification, as well as the Netscape and Internet Explorer release notes. Following the listing of HTML tags is a complete reference of all the named and numbered character entities for HTML. This listing is derived from the ISO 8859/1 Latin-1 character set.

Basic Document Tags

Tag	Description	Attributes
<BASE>	Used to specify the full URL of the current document.	HREF="..."
<BODY>...</BODY>	Tag pair for the body section of the HTML document. The body section includes all of the text and markup tags in the document.	BACKGROUND="..." BGCOLOR=... TEXT=... LINK=... ALINK=... VLINK=...
<HTML>...</HTML>	Tag pair for the entire HTML document.	PROMPT="..."
<ISINDEX>	Specifies to the server that this document can be searched.	
<HEAD>...</HEAD>	Tag pair for the head section of the HTML document.	
<TITLE>...</TITLE>	Specifies the title of the document.	

Style/Formatting Tags

Tag	Description	Attributes	Support Limited to
<A>...</A>	When used with the HREF attribute, inserts a hyperlink into your HTML document. When used with the NAME attribute, inserts an anchor into your HTML document. (In HTML3, use of the <A> tag with the NAME attribute has been phased out. Instead, you should use the ID element inside block elements.)	NAME="..." HREF="..."	
<ABBREV>... </ABBREV>	Indicates that the enclosed text is an abbreviation, and formats it accordingly.		HTML3
<ACRONYM>... </ACRONYM>	Indicates that the enclosed text is an acronym, and formats it accordingly.		HTML3
<B>...</B>	Displays the enclosed characters in boldface.		
<BASEFONT>	When used with the SIZE attribute, this tag overrides the default font size for the document. The font size can be any number from 1 to 7. The default is 3.	SIZE=...	
<BIG>...</BIG>	Displays the enclosed text in a larger font.		HTML3

Tag	Description	Attributes	Support Limited to
<BLINK>...</BLINK>	Causes the enclosed text to blink repeatedly. Known to cause unpredictable behavior in laboratory animals. Use with extreme caution.		Netscape
<CITE>...</CITE>	Formats the enclosed text in the logical citation style. This is used when you quote material from other works. Citation text is displayed by most browsers in italics.		
<CODE>...</CODE>	Formats the enclosed text as computer code. This is best used when you're showing examples of programming code. <CODE> text is displayed by most browsers in a monospaced font, such as Courier.		
<DEL>...</DEL>	The enclosed text is marked as deleted. This is generally used in legal documents or other material where it is necessary to display text that has been removed from the current version of a document.		HTML3
<DFN>...</DFN>	The enclosed text is the defining instance of a term or phrase.		HTML3
<EM>...</EM>	This logical markup tag instructs the browser to display the enclosed text with emphasis. Most browsers display <EM> text in italics.		
<FONT>...</FONT>	This tag allows you to specify font attributes for the enclosed text. The <FONT> tag was originally a Netscape extension, but it is now further extended by Internet Explorer as well.	COLOR=... FACE="..." SIZE=...	Netscape, Internet Explorer
<I>...</I>	Displays the enclosed text in italics.		HTML3
<INS>...</INS>	The enclosed text is marked as inserted. This is generally used in legal documents or other material where it is necessary to display text that has been added to the current version of a document.		
<KBD>...</KBD>	This logical markup tag is used to indicate that the enclosed text should be typed in by the reader exactly as shown.		
<PERSON>...</PERSON>	Marks names of people in text, allowing them to be highlighted. This tag is also used by some indexing programs to extract names from text.		HTML3

Tag	Description	Attributes	Support Limited to
<Q>...</Q>	Displays the enclosed text as a quotation. This is formatted by the browser appropriate to the context of the language used.		HTML3
<SAMP>...</SAMP>	This logical markup tag instructs the browser to display the enclosed text in sample style. This style is used for example material in your document.		
<SMALL>... </SMALL>	Displays the enclosed text in a smaller font.		HTML3
<STRIKE>... </STRIKE>	Displays the enclosed text in strike-through style, which places a horizontal line through the middle of the text.		
<STRONG>... </STRONG>	This logical markup tag instructs the browser to display the enclosed text with strong emphasis. Most browsers display <STRONG> text in bold.		
_{...}	Displays the enclosed text in subscript, placing it slightly below the current line.		Netscape, HTML3
^{...}	Displays the enclosed text in superscript, placing it slightly above the current line.		Netscape, HTML3
<TT>...</TT>	Displays the enclosed text in typewriter style. This is displayed by most browsers in a monospaced font.		
<VAR>...</VAR>	This logical style is used to indicate variables, which are items to be supplied by the reader of the document.		

Block Elements

Tag	Description	Attributes	Support Limited to
<ADDRESS>... </ADDRESS>	The enclosed text is defined as specific address information, and is often used to indicate such information as e-mail address, signature, or authorship of the document. The <ADDRESS> information usually appears at the very top or bottom of the HTML document. Most browsers display <ADDRESS> information in italics. The address element implies a paragraph break before and after.		

Tag	Description	Attributes	Support Limited to
<BLOCKQUOTE>… </BLOCKQUOTE>	Used to mark a section (block) of text as a quote from another source. <BLOCKQUOTE> text is indented and spaced apart from the current paragraph by most browsers.		
 …</BR>	Inserts a line break at a specific point in the document.		
<CENTER>… </CENTER>	Everything between these tags is centered in the document.		Netscape
<H1>…</H1>	Creates a headline. The number following the H can have a value from 1 to 6, with 1 creating the largest headline.	ALIGN=…	
<HR>…</HR>	Places a horizontal rule across the document.	NOSHADE SIZE=… WIDTH=…	
<MARQUEE>… </MARQUEE>	Inserts a scrolling text marquee in the document.	BEHAVIOR=… BGCOLOR=… DIRECTION=… HEIGHT=… LOOP=… SCROLLAMOUNT=… SCROLLDELAY=… WIDTH=…	Internet Explorer
<P>…</P>	Places a paragraph inside the document. The closing </P> tag is optional, but highly recommended, especially with HTML3.	ALIGN=… ID="…"	
<PRE>…</PRE>	The enclosed text is preformatted. It is displayed in a monospaced font exactly as it appears in the HTML source code.		

Form Elements

Tag	Description	Attributes	Support Limited to
<FORM>… </FORM>	Inserts an input form into the HTML document. Used to define an area containing input fields for user feedback. The two attributes, ACTION and METHOD, are required.	ACTION=… METHOD=…	

Tag	Description	Attributes	Support Limited to
<INPUT>	Inserts an input field in the form. The type of input field is determined using the TYPE attribute. Acceptable values for TYPE are TEXT, CHECKBOX, RADIO, SUBMIT, RESET, and HIDDEN.	CHECKED MAXLENGTH=… NAME=… SIZE=… TYPE=… VALUE=…	
<OPTION>…</OPTION>	Defines an item for a SELECT input object.	SELECTED	
<SELECT>…</SELECT>	Inserts a selection input object, pop-up menu.	MULTIPLE NAME=… SIZE=…	
<TEXTAREA>…</TEXTAREA>	Inserts a multiline text input field.	COLS=… NAME=… ROWS=…	

Hypertext Link Elements

Tag	Description	Attributes	Support Limited to
<A>…</A>	Marks the beginning and end of a hypertext link. Also used by earlier versions of HTML to mark an anchor by using the NAME attribute. Although still supported by HTML3, this use of the <A> and </A> tag pair has been superseded by the ID attribute.	HREF=… NAME=…	
<AREA>	Defines a clickable region inside a client-side image map.	COORDS=x,y,x,y HREF=… NOHREF SHAPE=…	
<MAP>…</MAP>	Defines a client-side image map.	NAME=…	

Image and Sound Tags

Tag	Description	Attributes	Support Limited to
<BGSOUND>	Instructs the browser to play a sound or music file (.WAV or MIDI format) in the background.	LOOP=… SRC="…"	Internet Explorer
<IMG>	Inserts an inline image into the HTML document.	ALIGN=… ALT="…" BORDER=… CONTROLS DYNSRC="…" HEIGHT=… HSPACE=… ISMAP LOOP=… SRC="…" START=… USEMAP VSPACE=… WIDTH=…	HTML3, Netscape, Internet Explorer

List Elements

Tag	Description	Attributes
<DD>…</DD>	Inserts a definition description into a <DL> definition list. Used in conjunction with a <DT>…</DT> tag pair.	
<DL>…</DL>	Inserts a definition list into the HTML document. Use the <DD> and <DT> tags to insert list items.	
<DT>…</DT>	Inserts a definition title into a <DL> definition list. Used in conjunction with a <DD>…</DD> tag pair.	
<LI>…</LI>	List item. Used with both ordered and unordered lists. The closing </LI> tag is optional.	SKIP=… (for ordered lists only)
<OL>…</OL>	Ordered list. Creates a list with items presented in sequential order.	SEQNUM=… TYPE=… CONTINUE
<UL>…</UL>	Unordered list. Creates a bulleted list of items presented in no particular order.	TYPE=…

Table Elements

Tag	Description	Attributes	Support Limited to
<CAPTION>...</CAPTION>	Inserts a caption for the table.	ALIGN=...	HTML3
<TABLE>...</TABLE>	Inserts a table in the HTML document.	BGCOLOR=... BORDER=... BORDERCOLOR=... BORDERCOLORDARK=... BORDERCOLORLIGHT=... WIDTH=... CELLSPACING=... CELLPADDING=...	HTML3, Netscape, Internet Explorer
<TD>...</TD>	Inserts a table data cell.	BGCOLOR=... ROWSPAN=... COLSPAN=... ALIGN=... VALIGN=...	HTML3, Netscape, Internet Explorer
<TH>...</TH>	Inserts a table header cell. The text contained inside is usually displayed in bold and is centered inside the cell.	BGCOLOR=... ROWSPAN=... COLSPAN=... ALIGN=... VALIGN=...	HTML3, Netscape, Internet Explorer
<TR>...</TR>	Defines a table row. All of the <TD>.and <TH> tags enclosed will appear in the same row of the table.	ALIGN=... BGCOLOR=... VALIGN=...	HTML3, Netscape, Internet Explorer

Character Entities

Commonly Used Characters

Entity	Description	Example
©	copyright symbol	©
®	registered trademark symbol	®
™	trademark symbol	™
	nonbreaking space	
<	less-than symbol	<
>	greater-than symbol	>
&	ampersand	&
"	quotation mark	"

Latin 1 Character Set (Named Character Entities)

This list is derived from the ISO 8859/1 character set. All of the entity names are case-sensitive.

Entity	Description	Example
Á	Capital A, acute accent	Á
À	Capital A, grave accent	À
Â	Capital A, circumflex accent	Â
Ã	Capital A, tilde	Ã
Å	Capital A, ring	Å
Ä	Capital A, dieresis or umlaut mark	Ä
Æ	Capital AE dipthong (ligature)	Æ
Ç	Capital C, cedilla	Ç
É	Capital E, acute accent	É
È	Capital E, grave accent	È
Ê	Capital E, circumflex accent	Ê
Ë	Capital E, dieresis or umlaut mark	Ë
Í	Capital I, acute accent	Í
Ì	Capital I, grave accent	Ì
Î	Capital I, circumflex accent	Î
Ï	Capital I, dieresis or umlaut mark	Ï
Ð	Capital Eth, Icelandic	

Entity	Description	Example
Ñ	Capital N, tilde	Ñ
Ó	Capital O, acute accent	Ó
Ò	Capital O, grave accent	Ò
Ô	Capital O, circumflex accent	Ô
&Otilde	Capital O, tilde	Õ
Ö	Capital O, dieresis or umlaut mark	Ö
&Oslash	Capital O, slash	Ø
Ú	Capital U, acute accent	Ú
Ù	Capital U, grave accent	Ù
Û	Capital U, circumflex accent	Û
Ü	Capital U, dieresis or umlaut mark	Ü
Ý	Capital Y, acute accent	Ý
Þ	Capital THORN, Icelandic	
á	Small a, acute accent	á
à	Small a, grave accent	à
â	Small a, circumflex accent	â
ã	Small a, tilde	ã
ä	Small a, dieresis or umlaut mark	ä
æ	Small ae dipthong (ligature)	æ
ç	Small c, cedilla	ç
é	Small e, acute accent	é
è	Small e, grave accent	è
ê	Small e, circumflex accent	ê
ë	Small e, dieresis or umlaut mark	ë
í	Small i, acute accent	í
ì	Small i, grave accent	ì
î	Small i, circumflex accent	î
ï	Small i, dieresis or umlaut mark	ï
ð	Small eth, Icelandic	ð
&ntilde	Small n, tilde	ñ
ó	Small o, acute accent	ó
ò	Small o, grave accent	ò
ô	Small o, circumflex accent	ô
õ	Small o, tilde	õ

Entity	Description	Example
ö	Small o, dieresis or umlaut mark	ö
&oslash	Small o, slash	ø
ß	Small sharp s, German (sz ligature)	ß
&uacute	Small u, acute accent	ú
&ugrave	Small u, grave accent	ù
û	Small u, circumflex accent	û
ü	Small u, dieresis or umlaut mark	ü
&yacute	Small y, acute accent	ý
þ	Small thorn, Icelandic	
ÿ	Small y, dieresis or umlaut mark	ÿ

Numbered Character Entities

Entity	Description	Example
&#01; - &#08;	Unused	
		Horizontal tab	

	Line feed	

&#11; - &#31;	Unused	
 	Space	
!	Exclamation mark	!
"	Quotation mark	"
#	Number sign	#
$	Dollar sign	$
%	Percent sign	%
&	Ampersand	&
'	Apostrophe	'
(	Left parenthesis	(
)	Right parenthesis	)
*	Asterisk	*
+	Plus sign	+
,	Comma	,
-	Hyphen	-
.	Period	.
/	Forward slash	/
0 - 9	Digits 0–9	

Entity	Description	Example
&#58;	Colon	:
&#59;	Semicolon	;
&#60;	Less-than symbol	<
&#61;	Equal sign	=
&#62;	Greater-than symbol	>
&#63;	Question mark	?
&#64;	Commercial at	@
A - Z	Letters A–Z	
&#91;	Left square bracket	[
&#92;	Reverse solidus (backslash)	\
&#93;	Right square bracket	]
&#94;	Circumflex	^
&#95;	Horizontal bar	_
&#96;	Grave accent	`
a - z	Letters a–z	'
&#123;	Left curly brace	{
|	Vertical bar	|
&#125;	Right curly brace	}
&#126;	Tilde	~
&#127; -	Unused	
&#161;	Inverted exclamation	¡
&#162;	Cent sign	¢
&#163;	Pound sterling	£
&#164;	General currency sign	¤
&#165;	Yen sign	¥
&#166;	Broken vertical bar (pipe symbol)	¦
&#167;	Section sign	§
&#168;	Umlaut (dieresis)	¨
&#169;	Copyright	©
&#170;	Feminine ordinal	ª
&#171;	Left angle quote, guillemotleft	«
&#172;	Not sign	¬
&#173;	Soft hyphen	–
&#174;	Registered trademark	®

Entity	Description	Example
¯	Macron accent	¯
°	Degree sign	°
±	Plus or minus	±
²	Superscript two	2
³	Superscript three	3
´	Acute accent	´
µ	Micro sign	μ
¶	Paragraph sign	¶
·	Middle dot	·
¸	Cedilla	¸
¹	Superscript one	1
º	Masculine ordinal	º
»	Right angle quote, guillemotright	»
¼	Fraction one-fourth	¼
½	Fraction one-half	½
¾	Fraction three-fourths	¾
¿	Inverted question mark	¿
À	Capital A, grave accent	À
Á	Capital A, acute accent	Á
Â	Capital A, circumflex accent	Â
Ã	Capital A, tilde	Ã
Ä	Capital A, ring	Å
Å	Capital A, dieresis or umlaut mark	Ä
Æ	Capital AE dipthong (ligature)	Æ
Ç	Capital C, cedilla	Ç
È	Capital E, grave accent	È
É	Capital E, acute accent	É
Ê	Capital E, circumflex accent	Ê
Ë	Capital E, dieresis or umlaut mark	Ë
Ì	Capital I, grave accent	Ì
Í	Capital I, acute accent	Í
Î	Capital I, circumflex accent	Î
Ï	Capital I, dieresis or umlaut mark	Ï
Ð	Capital Eth, Icelandic	

Entity	Description	Example
Ñ	Capital N, tilde	Ñ
Ò	Capital O, grave accent	Ò
Ó	Capital O, acute accent	Ó
Ô	Capital O, circumflex accent	Ô
Õ	Capital O, tilde	Õ
Ö	Capital O, dieresis or umlaut mark	Ö
×	Multiplication sign	x
Ø	Capital O, slash	Ø
Ù	Capital U, grave accent	Ù
Ú	Capital U, acute accent	Ú
Û	Capital U, circumflex accent	Û
Ü	Capital U, dieresis or umlaut mark	Ü
Ý	Capital Y, acute accent	Ý
Þ	Capital THORN, Icelandic	
ß	Small sharp s, German (sz ligature)	ß
à	Small a, grave accent	à
á	Small a, acute accent	á
â	Small a, circumflex accent	â
ã	Small a, tilde	ã
ä	Small a, ring	å
å	Small a, dieresis or umlaut mark	ä
æ	Small ae dipthong (ligature)	æ
ç	Small c, cedilla	ç
è	Small e, grave accent	è
é	Small e, acute accent	é
ê	Small e, circumflex accent	ê
ë	Small e, dieresis or umlaut mark	ë
ì	Small i, grave accent	ì
í	Small i, acute accent	í
î	Small i, circumflex accent	î
ï	Small i, dieresis or umlaut mark	ï
ð	Small eth, Icelandic	∂
ñ	Small n, tilde	ñ
ò	Small o, grave accent	ò

Entity	Description	Example
ó	Small o, acute accent	ó
ô	Small o, circumflex accent	ô
õ	Small o, tilde	õ
ö	Small o, dieresis or umlaut mark	ö
÷	Division sign	÷
ø	Small o, slash	ø
ù	Small u, grave accent	ù
ú	Small u, acute accent	ú
û	Small u, circumflex accent	û
ü	Small u, dieresis or umlaut mark	ü
ý	Small y, acute accent	ý
þ	Small thorn, Icelandic	
ÿ	Small y, dieresis or umlaut mark	ÿ

CREDITS

We would like to thank the following individuals and companies whose content appears in *How to Use HTML3*:

Eve Andersson (Eve Andersson's Home Page)

Ziff-Davis Interactive (ZD Net Web site; ZD Net 3D VRML site)

Cleveland Indians (The Cleveland Indians Team Shop Web Page)

Lawrence Berkeley National Laboratory (The Virtual Frog Dissection Kit)

Nesbitt Software (Web edit v1.4)

Media Shower, Inc. (ZUG Home Page)

Silicon Graphics (The Impressionist)

Darrick Brown (LED Sign Java application)

Luis Fernandes (The Abacus: The Art of Calculating with Beads)

INDEX